~FERRIES O... PORTSM...
and The S...nt

CW00525777

Miles Cowsill

ISBN: 1 871947 28 6
Published by

12 Millfields Close, Kilgetty, Pembrokeshire, Wales SA68 0SA
Tel: (01834) 813991 Fax: (01834) 814484

The *Viking I* in the Solent in the Sixties. *(Ferry Publications Library)*

ACKNOWLEDGEMENTS

I would like to extend firstly my thanks to Rear Admiral George for agreeing to write the Foreword to this title. I am also indebted to Dick Martin, Managing Director, P&O European Ferries (Portsmouth) Limited; Ian Carruthers, Managing Director, Brittany Ferries (UK & Ireland); Jeff Vidamour, Managing Director, Commodore Ferries; Mel Williams, Managing Director, Wightlink; Gareth Cooper, Managing Director, Stena Sealink Line and Alistair Whyte, Managing Director, Red Funnel Group for agreeing to contribute and support this title.

I am indebted to my good friends Captain Bertrand Apperry, Senior Master of the ***Normandie*** and Tony Shopland, Senior Master of the ***Pride of Portsmouth*** for their valuable contributions to this book. My thanks also to Andrew Munn for his chapter.

I would also like to thank the following for their assistance with information and photographs for this publication:

Richard Kirkman (P&O European Ferries); Penny Guy (P&O European Ferries); Toby Oliver (Brittany Ferries Information Bureau); Jill Adams (Wightlink); Olive Glass (Red Funnel Ferries); Mike Archibald (Acadia Communications); Jim Hannah, Brian Rees and Chris Laming (Stena Sealink Line); Phil Neumann (FotoFlite); David Marshall, Eric Brett, Mark Willis and Gary Davies (Maritime Photographic).

I would like to thank my good friend and partner in Ferry Publications, John Hendy for his constructive comments and suggestions during its preparation. Thanks to Pat Somner and my wife Linda for their observations and comments. Finally, I would like to thank Ian Smith at Bèzier Design and Haven Colourprint for the high quality production of this book.

© Ferry Publications 1995

CONTENTS

The ***Armorique*** leaving Portsmouth for St. Malo in June 1985. *(Miles Cowsill)*

FOREWORD

The development of the Continental Ferry Port at Portsmouth from its standing start in 1976 has been dramatic and the growth in traffic using the ferry port has been relentless through the intervening years. Portsmouth is a unique example of a burgeoning municipal port, owned and operated by the City Council for the benefit not only of those that use the port but also for the citizens of Portsmouth who share in the employment and prosperity that it brings.

I am delighted that Miles Cowsill has turned his talents towards the ferries that use this port as these, too, have followed the pattern of growth. When looking at the current generation of luxurious superferries with their huge capacity and superb facilities, it is difficult to remember the ferries that first used this port. Then, they seemed to be the last word in ferry technology and comfort; now they appear to be puny and old fashioned. It is good, however, that they will be remembered in this book, as it will provide a yardstick against which progress to date can be measured.

The ferry industry faces an uncertain future not only with the opening of the Channel Tunnel but also with the rapidly developing technology in fast ferries. Portsmouth is well prepared as it was the base for the first cross-channel fast ferry service and gained invaluable experience which will be put to good use when these ferries return here. Meanwhile we are a Quality Assured Port from where superferries, offering a 5-star service, operate; the combination setting new standards for the industry and giving our passengers and freight customers what I hope will prove to be an irresistible alternative to the Channel Tunnel in the years to come.

Rear Admiral Tony George

Portsmouth and its ferries are in good shape as will be evident from this fascinating book.

Rear Admiral Tony George
January 1995

"Seems Mole's got Tunnel vision again."

(In the style of E H Shepard, by permission of Shepard Estate)

"He never could resist a new tunnel" said Rat, with more than a hint of disapproval in his voice. "Only trouble is, he's not only had to go out of his way to get there, but when he reaches the other side he'll be nowhere near his final destination".

Anyone moving freight abroad can see from a glance at the map that Portsmouth is remarkably well situated for their purposes.

And this isn't just because of the City's central position on England's South Coast, which has long made it the natural gateway to continental Europe. It's also because of Portsmouth's fast, modern road links, on both sides of the Channel. On this side, only yards away from the Port Terminal, is the M275 which connects directly to the M27 and the rest of Britain's motorway network. (Portsmouth is actually closer than Dover to London.)

On the other side, Portsmouth's six cross-Channel routes take you closer to almost anywhere in France, Spain, Portugal, Italy and the Med. Of course when you sail from Portsmouth, you take your rest break on board a ferry, in the luxury of one of the vessels operated by P&O or Brittany Ferries. How much better relaxing at sea than messing about in tunnels and laybys; that is, unless you're a mole!

Brittany Ferries
The Holiday Fleet

P&O
European Ferries

PORTSMOUTH
CROSS CHANNEL PORT

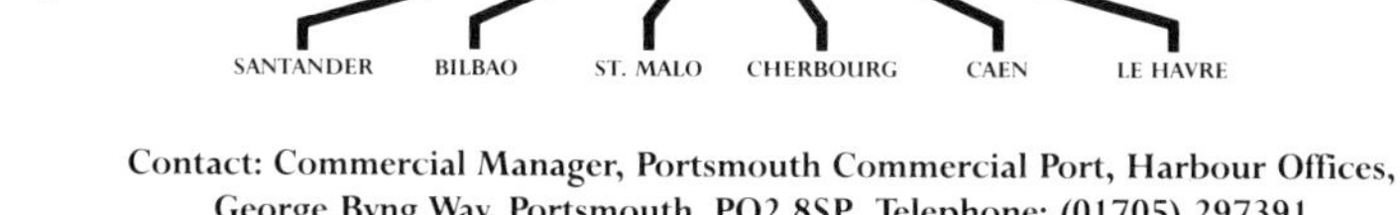

Contact: Commercial Manager, Portsmouth Commercial Port, Harbour Offices, George Byng Way, Portsmouth, PO2 8SP. Telephone: (01705) 297391

Brittany Ferries, Tel: (01202) 441100 *Caen St. Malo Santander*
P&O European Ferries (Portsmouth) Ltd., Tel: (01705) 772332 *Cherbourg Le Havre Bilbao*

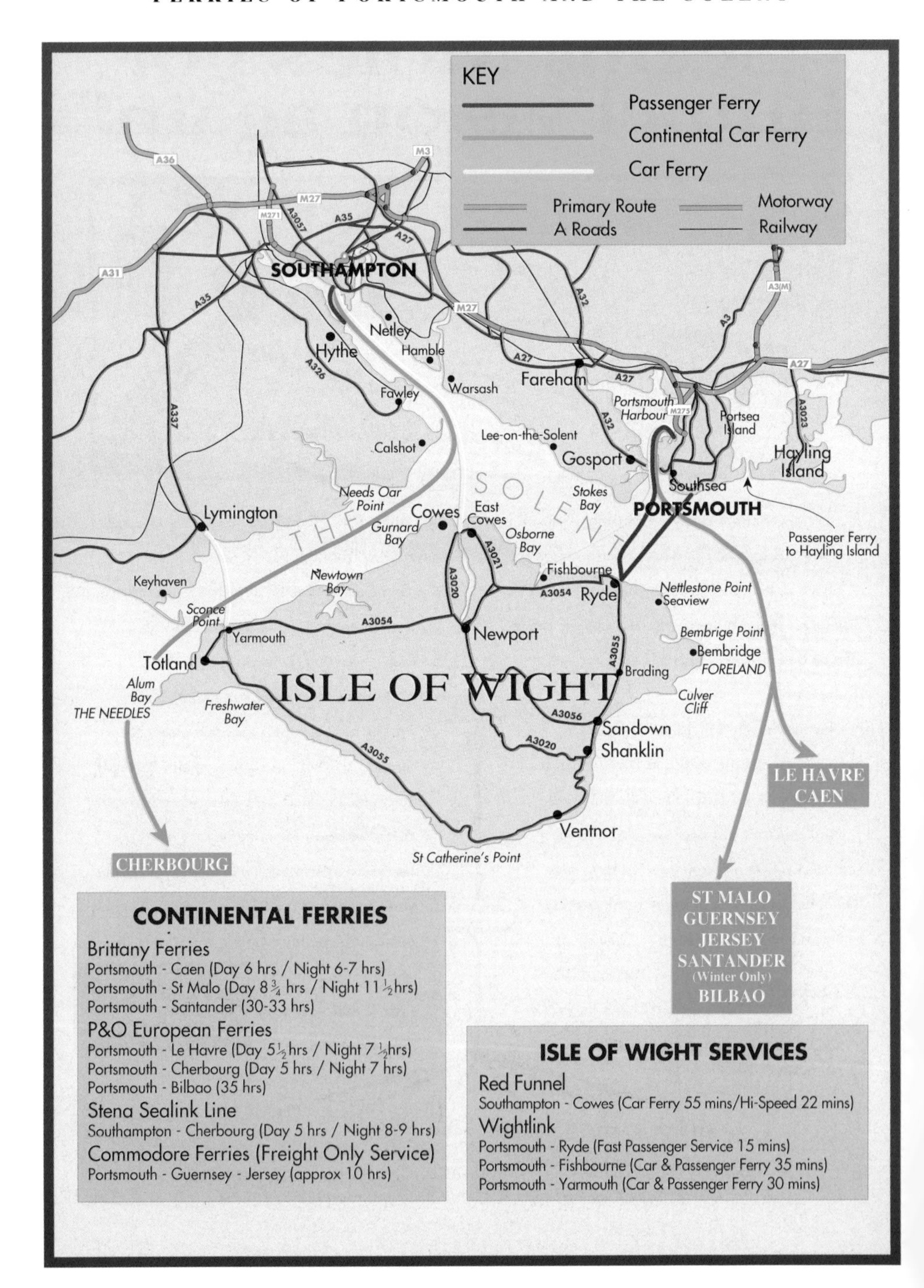
KEY
Passenger Ferry
Continental Car Ferry
Car Ferry
Primary Route
A Roads
Motorway
Railway
A36
M3
M27
M271
A3057
A35
A27
A31
SOUTHAMPTON
A35
M27
A32
A3(M)
A3
A27
Netley
Hythe
Hamble
A326
Fawley
Warsash
Fareham
A27
A337
Portsmouth Harbour
M275
A32
Portsea Island
A3023
Lee-on-the-Solent
Calshot
Gosport
Hayling Island
Southsea
Needs Oar Point
THE SOLENT
Stokes Bay
PORTSMOUTH
Lymington
Cowes
East Cowes
Gurnard Bay
Osborne Bay
A3021
Passenger Ferry to Hayling Island
Keyhaven
Newtown Bay
A3020
Fishbourne
A3054
Ryde
Nettlestone Point
Seaview
Sconce Point
Yarmouth
A3054
Newport
Bembrige Point
Bembridge
FORELAND
A3055
Brading
Totland
Alum Bay
THE NEEDLES
ISLE OF WIGHT
Freshwater Bay
Culver Cliff
A3056
Sandown
A3020
Shanklin
A3055
LE HAVRE
CAEN
Ventnor
CHERBOURG
St Catherine's Point
ST MALO
GUERNSEY
JERSEY
SANTANDER
(Winter Only)
BILBAO
CONTINENTAL FERRIES
Brittany Ferries
Portsmouth - Caen (Day 6 hrs / Night 6-7 hrs)
Portsmouth - St Malo (Day 8¾ hrs / Night 11½hrs)
Portsmouth - Santander (30-33 hrs)
P&O European Ferries
Portsmouth - Le Havre (Day 5½ hrs / Night 7½hrs)
Portsmouth - Cherbourg (Day 5 hrs / Night 7 hrs)
Portsmouth - Bilbao (35 hrs)
Stena Sealink Line
Southampton - Cherbourg (Day 5 hrs / Night 8-9 hrs)
Commodore Ferries (Freight Only Service)
Portsmouth - Guernsey - Jersey (approx 10 hrs)
ISLE OF WIGHT SERVICES
Red Funnel
Southampton - Cowes (Car Ferry 55 mins/Hi-Speed 22 mins)
Wightlink
Portsmouth - Ryde (Fast Passenger Service 15 mins)
Portsmouth - Fishbourne (Car & Passenger Ferry 35 mins)
Portsmouth - Yarmouth (Car & Passenger Ferry 30 mins)

INTRODUCTION

With the opening of the Channel Tunnel and the possible decline in ferry operations on the Dover Straits in the next couple of years, Portsmouth and Southampton are set to become the main focus of ferry operations to France and Spain from the UK. In the light of the fixed link, all the continental ferry operators on the Western Channel have geared themselves up to compete with Eurotunnel, with ferries in most cases which can only be described as mini-liners.

Barring a bridge to the Isle of Wight, the ferry operators to the Island should also continue to prosper. Again, there has been major investment in the last couple of years by both Red Funnel and Wightlink to meet the ever higher standards required by the travelling public.

This book covers the history of the development of continental ferry services from Portsmouth and Southampton. The title also covers a brief history of the ferry services offered from Lymington, Southampton and Portsmouth to the Isle of Wight, and a look at the other ferry operators on the Solent which are so vital to the economy of the area.

I have witnessed with great interest the expansion of the ferry operations at Portsmouth and on the Solent during the last thirty years, it has been a fascinating period of rapid development. The demand by the travelling public to go further afield over the next ten years will possibly see the ports of Portsmouth and Southampton reaching as far as Portugal and Northern Africa.

Whilst liner travel in most cases is a thing of a life-time for most of us, travelling on a ferry is very accessible in the nineties and gives an opportunity to cruise in style, whether on the Solent or on the English Channel.

Miles Cowsill
March 1995

The ***Reine Mathilde*** arriving at Portsmouth. *(Miles Cowsill)*

PORTSMOUTH COMMERCIAL DOCKS

HISTORY AND BACKGROUND

Portsmouth has a fine natural harbour whose entrance is well protected from the prevailing winds by the Isle of Wight. Its short sea approaches and internal channels need little dredging and give easy access to the English Channel, bypassing the now crowded waters of the Solent. It is located in a central and commanding position in the centre of the south Coast of England, convenient for many of the northern French ports.

In consequence the harbour has been in continuous commercial use since Roman times with the commercial development of the port going hand in hand with the development of the naval port.

Commercial activities for many centuries were centred on the Camber situated close to the harbour mouth and by the 19th century the port extended from Emsworth to Hill Head. But it was not until 1839 that the Town Council promoted an Act of Parliament which created the municipal port. In 1868 Flathouse Quay in the Fountain Lake area was added to the municipal port to contain the overflow from the Camber. Later, in 1968, the City Council built Albert Johnson Quay on reclaimed land just to the north of Flathouse. Both these quays have recently been improved and deepened to take deep draft fruit and

The ***Viking I*** (later renamed ***Viking Victory***) undertaking berthing trials in May 1976 at Berth No 1 at the Continental Ferry Port. *(Portsmouth City Council)*

banana ships. They are well provided with temperature-controlled warehouses in which to store fruit. Their development has enabled Portsmouth to become the largest fruit importing port in the UK.

In the 1970s one or two ferry companies encouraged the City Council to construct a ferry port which was completed in 1976. The short sea approaches, Portsmouth's location with respect to the northern French ports and its unrivalled road access ensured instant success. From the beginning there has been a tremendous growth in passenger and freight traffic. Portsmouth is closer to London than Dover or the Channel Tunnel and the continental ferry port has a motorway right up to its entrance gate. Road communications to the Midlands, North and West avoiding London are simple, direct and give short journey times, thus making it very attractive not only for ferry passengers bound for France, Italy and the Iberian Peninsula, but also for freight wishing to connect with continental motorways. To meet this growth the Continental Ferry Port has been expanded and developed in several phases, the last of which, Phase VI, was opened in September 1991 and provided the finishing touches to the present up-to-date effective and efficient continental ferry port.

The Continental Ferry Port in the next stage of development in 1983. *(Portsmouth City Council)*

The Continental Ferry Port and Albert Johnson Quay in 1978. *(Portsmouth City Council)*

PRESENT POSITION

The commercial port has now become something of a cuckoo in the nest in the old naval port. Commercial shipping now represents two thirds of the total ship movements in the harbour and the commercial docks' turnover is set to reach £15m this year A new and successful pilotage service for commercial ships was set up by the City Council in 1988 as the result of legislation that saw the end of the UK-wide pilotage service provided until then by Trinity House. There are four pilots with two modern pilot boats who

The **Normandie** and **Armorique** pass each in June 1992. *(Brittany Ferries)*

fully meet the needs of commercial shipping. The Queen's Harbour Master remains responsible overall for controlling ship movements and for the safety of navigation within the port. In this way the naval and commercial shipping is subject to a single control, and both activities combine well together within the harbour.

The Continental Ferry Port now extends to 29 acres. It has four roll-on roll-off berths and provides everything necessary for passengers, passenger cars, coaches, caravans and freight. It is used by P&O European Ferries who operate services to and from Le Havre, Cherbourg and Bilbao. It is also used by Brittany Ferries who also run services to and from Caen, St.Malo and Santander; and Commodore who run freight only services to the Channel Islands. Currently about 3 million passengers, 900,000 cars and 300,000 freight units use the Ferry Port annually. Past rapid growth in this traffic, although welcome, gave rise to congestion; the opening of Phase VI cured this congestion by providing more space and better facilities. Current growth has caused the City Council to expand the ferry port again by the acquisition of extra land and a further reclamation scheme is planned for construction in 1995.

Brittany Ferries' *Normandie*, the first of the new generation of superferries, started service at Portsmouth in 1992. She was the forerunner of several new and larger ferries which include Brittany Ferries' *Bretagne*, on the St.Malo route, and *Val de Loire*, which operates between Portsmouth and Santander in the winter months. In 1993 P&O introduced the *Pride of Bilbao*, which is the largest ferry operating out of the UK and which has very successfully pioneered a new route between Portsmouth and Bilbao in Northern Spain. More recently P&O have introduced two more superferries, the

Pride of Winchester (FotoFlite)

An artist's impression of the new Commodore Ferries vessel which is due to enter service between Portsmouth and the Channel Islands in May 1995. *(Commodore Ferries)*

Pride of Portsmouth and the *Pride of Le Havre,* on their Le Havre service and have upgraded their ships running to and from Cherbourg. Overall the combination of quality of ships and the quality of the port are unrivalled by any other UK port.

Portsmouth has proved to be a unique and interesting example of a successful municipal port. It has demonstrated that local government can develop and run a successful commercial enterprise, despite the restrictions placed upon its borrowing and investment by central government. These constraints, which have recently become very much more stringent, have caused the City Council to invest substantial capital in the ferry port from the sale of assets. These investments provide for greatly improved facilities for both passenger and freight.

THE FUTURE

The future strategy for the commercial docks relates mostly to the Continental Ferry Port which now generates more than three quarters of the commercial docks' total income. The Channel Tunnel therefore looms large. In considering its effect on Portsmouth it seems likely that departure point and destination are still going to determine travellers' choice of port and current experience suggests that the tunnel will not only help to enlarge the total cross-channel market, but also will tend to take from Dover, leaving Portsmouth's market share more or less unscathed. Overall over-capacity is likely to destabilise prices throughout the cross-channel market and drive them downwards, at least until capacity is brought into line with demand again.

The ferry companies' reaction to the threat of the tunnel is to provide a better quality of service at a lower ticket price. To achieve that, the ferry companies are bringing in larger ships, which are cheaper to run in unit cost terms. For these lower unit costs to be realised, the ships have to be filled and higher volumes have to be carried which, at a time when the Channel Tunnel is about to open, is bound to affect prices. These bigger ships have better onboard retail services through which the ferry companies hope to recoup overall passenger revenues.

Bigger ships and higher volume of passengers and freight will call for significant expansion and improvement of berths for the larger ships and space for the higher volumes. Also passenger expectations are always rising, with the consequence that improved facilities for passengers and freight drivers will have to be provided in the port whose services are now quality assured to BS5750.

But underlying any short-term problems is the knowledge that there is enormous potential growth in both the freight and passenger markets. EU development will provide the former, and the growing wish among holiday makers to take their car, to visit the EC and to travel in Europe avoiding the high cost and possible disruption of long-distance flights, assures us of the latter. The Channel Tunnel itself will give a boost to the travel market, and the fact that Portsmouth is easy to reach, provides a variety of destinations in France with a 4-5 hour enjoyable crossing and above all is closer to virtually all centres of population in the UK than the Tunnel at Folkestone, will assure our future business.

The ***Bretagne*** seen loading at Portsmouth. *(Brittany Ferries)*

CONTINENTAL FERRY OPERATIONS

SOUTHAMPTON

The port of Southampton was once referred to by Sir Herbert Walker, then Chairman of its owners, as "the jewel in the crown of the Southern Railway".

Whilst the history of the port of Southampton stretches back many centuries, the real development of the commercial shipping and cargo handling facilities in Southampton has taken place only during the last 156 years. Southampton's good geographical location and natural deep water have always been a significant attraction. The port for many has been the gateway to a new world in the era of the British empire and it also was, until the advancement of the jet airliner, the main route to the Americas.

Southampton was not only an international liner port, but was also an important terminus for cross-channel ferries for British Rail for their passenger services to the Channel Islands, St.Malo and Le Havre until the early sixties. The ferry services to these destinations were operated from the outer dock at the port by famous steamers such as the *Normannia*, *Isle of Guernsey* and *Falaise*. In 1961 British Railways decided that their passenger services to the Channel Islands would be transferred to Weymouth, and so the Southampton-Channel Islands passenger services came to an end with the last arrival of the *Isle of Guernsey* on 12th May 1961. Three years later, on 9th May 1964, the Le Havre service was closed, and some four months later, on 27th September, the St. Malo link was also closed down, thus ending all British Railways' passenger sailings from the port. The cargo service for the Channel Islands remained operative until 1972 when it was transferred to Portsmouth.

In the light of the rundown of operations by British Railways, an entrepreneur from Norway decided to open his own service from Southampton to the ports of Cherbourg and Le Havre. To enable the Norwegian to start his new operation, work began in February 1963 on developing the inner dock at Southampton to provide a linkspan and passenger halls for the new operation.

In the meantime Otto Thoresen placed

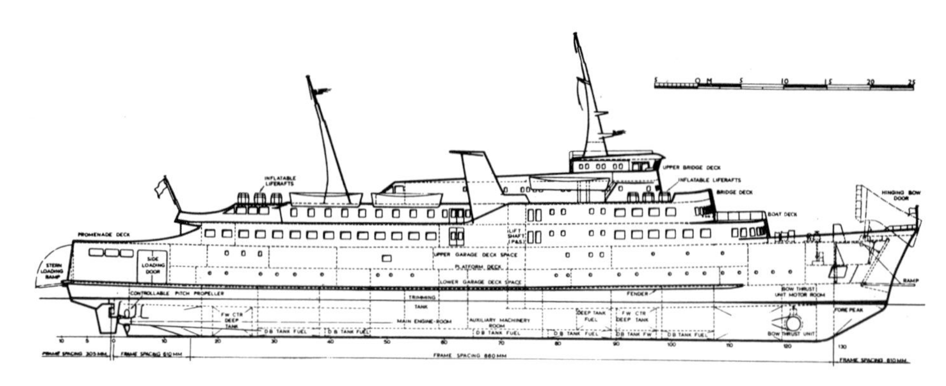

Cross section of ***Viking I.*** *(Ferry Publications Library)*

The ***Car Ferry Viking I*** at Southampton prior to her inaugural voyage to Cherbourg. *(Ferry Publications Library)*

an order for the first of his new revolutionary drive on-drive off ferries which would be able to carry 180 cars on two decks. At Southampton the ship would load stern in, and cars would drive off at the bow in France, the first drive-through ships to serve our shores. The vessel would have passenger accommodation for 940 passengers, with 300 berths for overnight accommodation.

The strength of early bookings and the tremendous enthusiasm on both sides of the English Channel encouraged Otto Thoresen to order a second vessel. It is interesting to note that the first of his ships cost only £1.2 million each.

It was announced in November 1963 that the two new ferries would be named *Viking I* and *Viking II*, and the first of the ships to be delivered would start commercial service on 11th May 1964, while the second ship would start in the August.

The *Viking I's* keel was laid in October 1963, and she entered the icy waters of the fjord for the first time shortly before noon the following January, just 18 weeks later. She was delivered by the Norwegian yard on 29th April, and achieved on her trials 20.5 knots, one knot faster than her original design speed. Meanwhile, on 30th April, her sister, the *Viking II*, was launched.

The inaugural sailing between Southampton and Cherbourg by Thoresen Car Ferries, as it was to be known, was made by the *Viking I* on 11th May 1964. Some 170 cars were carried on the first five-hour crossing, which left Southampton at 10.30. With only one hour's turnround at Cherbourg, she left again at 16.30, returning to Southampton in the early evening. This pattern of sailings was to continue to the 15th May when some night sailings were introduced. During the first three operating weeks, Thoresen Car Ferries carried 13,000

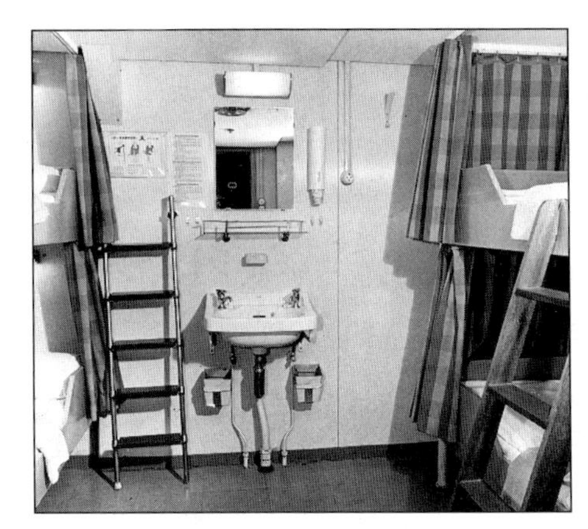

Left: The aft end of the promenade deck with aircraft seating and cabins, on the left, on board ***Viking I***. Right: The ***Viking II,*** like her sisters, offered excellent cabin accommodation, far ahead of the operators of the day. *(Ferry Publications Library)*

passengers and 3,500 cars. Bookings already showed that a profit would be made, yet British Railways had claimed that their services to France from Southampton lost them £173,116 a year. In the whole of 1962, British Rail had carried only 72,190 passengers and 2,642 cars. Otto Thoresen was quickly to show that a private operator could make money.

The *Viking II* entered service on 19th July 1964 and was transferred to the Cherbourg link, allowing the *Viking I* to formally open the Southampton-Le Havre service.

In July 1964, the decision was made by the Board of Directors of Thoresen Car Ferries, to order a third ferry for the following season. The order this time was made to a German shipyard. The new ferry

The ***Viking II*** seen arriving at Southampton in August 1964. *(R Sprake Collection)*

The ***Viking III*** was launched on 10th March 1965 at Lubeck in West Germany. *(Ferry Publications Library)*

would allow the company greater flexibility and would enable them to cope with the anticipated increase of traffic on both routes for the next season.

The company continued to expand, and in 1966 a fourth ship was ordered to handle freight between Southampton and Le Havre. The *Viking IV*, as she was to be named, entered service in 1967 and could accommodate 40 lorries, trailers or containers and 130 export cars.

The early successes of Thoresen Car Ferries tempted other shipping companies to explore services from the port. In April 1967, Swedish Lloyd opened a new ferry service with their *Patricia* to Bilbao in

A view of the Princess Alexandra Dock at Southampton showing the freight vessel ***Viking IV*** offloading straight onto the quay while ***Viking I*** awaits her night sailing to Le Havre. *(Ferry Publications Library)*

The British registered ***Dragon*** entered service between Southampton and Le Havre on 29th June 1967. She was joined by her French sister the ***Leopard*** during May 1968. *(FotoFlite)*

Northern Spain. Meanwhile, a subsidiary of P&O, the General Steam Navigation Company, had started a limited cargo service from Southampton to Le Havre. The success of Otto Thoresen's venture prompted them to enter into partnership with the French company SAGA and two vessels were ordered in France for delivery in 1967. The joint operation was to be known as Normandy Ferries and was to go into competition with Thoresen Car Ferries' earlier established service. Both ships were to cost just under £2 million each, and offered excellent accommodation for 850 passengers, but were only to be stern loading vessels, which could accommodate 250 cars. At 18 knots, both sisters, which were to be named *Dragon* and *Leopard*, were slightly slower than the Viking class ships operated by Thoresen Car Ferries.

The *Dragon* made her maiden voyage on 7th July 1967, and during her first season she offered a 22.30 sailing from Southampton with a return passage at 11.30 from Le Havre. On 19th May 1968, she was joined by the French registered *Leopard* on the link.

Both vessels of P&O were to offer additional services to that of Le Havre, including a ferry link between Le Havre and Rosslare. During the winter of 1968/69, the *Dragon* and later the *Leopard* offered sailings from Britain and France to Lisbon and Casablanca. So hopeful were P&O that these

In the summer of 1970, ***Free Enterprise II*** started her first season on the Western Channel operating between Southampton and Cherbourg. The former Dover vessel is seen here arriving at Portsmouth later in her career with Townsend Thoresen. *(Eric Brett)*

new services would be successful that, an order was made for a large new cruise ferry, the *Eagle*, which would be delivered in 1971. Until her delivery, the *Dragon* and *Leopard* continued their off-peak services to Lisbon and sometimes to Casablanca. The *Eagle* eventually entered service offering an all year round operation under the banner of P&O Southern Ferries.

Meanwhile, two further services were established during the late sixties to the Iberian Peninsula from Southampton. Swedish Lloyd had already started their operations in 1967, to be followed by Anzar Line with the *Monte Toledo* to Santander and P&O Southern Ferries, using the *SF Panther* to San Sebastian. All three companies failed to make the operations pay, with passengers having to spend some 37 hours at sea, which involved two nights on board on both passages. Swedish Lloyd and Anzar Line closed their services at the end of the summer in 1977. Meanwhile P&O Southern Ferries gave up their service in the previous year.

In 1968 the merger took place between the Dover based Townsend Car Ferries and Otto Thoresen's company, which was to create Britain's largest independent ferry company, European Ferries, trading as Townsend Thoresen. The operation at Southampton was to carry on very much as it had done in previous years, following the merger. The Dover and Southampton operations continued to operate as separate companies, apart from the marketing and brand name of the company, for the next couple of years. By 1972, the Townsend Thoresen name had been placed on the side of the hulls of all the vessels at Southampton in place of Thoresen Car Ferries, and the TTF logo also appeared on the funnels in pale green. By 1976 the Thoresen orange which had been introduced by Otto Thoresen as a safety measure was adopted throughout the fleet.

The launch of ***Viking Venturer*** at Aalborg Vaerft, Denmark on 1st June 1974. *(Ferry Publications Library)*

In the summer of 1970, Dover's *Free Enterprise II* started her first season on the Southampton-Cherbourg service, supporting the 'Viking' ferries. Whilst the Dover vessel offered additional capacity, she did not offer the same high standard of accommodation as the former Thoresen ships.

In December 1970, Townsend Thoresen announced a five year expansion programme with the construction of five new ships costing some £20 million. Two new 'Free Enterprise' class ships were ordered for Dover, whilst Southampton would have three 'Super Vikings' built in Denmark. In the event, Southampton was only to receive two 'Super Vikings', which would be able to accommodate 275 cars and 1,200 passengers. The first vessel to be delivered was to be named the *Viking Venturer*. She left Denmark under the command of Captain Tony Shopland in early January 1975 and entered service on 22nd January on the Le Havre service running in tandem with the *Viking III*, which allowed the *Viking I* to be transferred to the new Felixstowe-Zeebrugge service.

The second 'Super Viking' for Southampton, the *Viking Valiant*, was launched some three months earlier and entered operations on 21st May 1975 to join the *Viking II* on Zeebrugge service, allowing the *Viking I* to return to Southampton for the summer season.

A fourth 'Super Viking' was later ordered by the Company, and once the third 'Super Viking', the *Viking Viscount*, and fourth, *Viking Voyager*, had been delivered to the Company for the Zeebrugge operations, the *Viking Valiant* transferred to the Southampton-Le Havre link.

In the light of this expansion, Townsend Thoresen had been faced with a series of industrial disputes at Southampton. With the need for cost savings and to make greater use of the vessels in the fleet, it was decided to transfer some of their operations in 1976 to Portsmouth. The port not only saved an hour's sailing time, but also provided excellent road communications to London and the Midlands. With a spur of the M27 leading right to the newly established terminal, it offered a traffic free operation compared to that of Southampton. More importantly, perhaps, Portsmouth lacked the fierce and militant trade union practices which were now beginning to strangle Southampton. In April 1976, Townsend Thoresen announced that they would open a new ferry service between Portsmouth and Cherbourg between the 17th June and 12th September, leaving at 08.00 with the return at 14.00 each day. Night sailings,

The ***Viking Venturer*** was the first of the 'Super Viking' class ships to enter operations at Southampton in January 1975. *(Ferry Publications Library)*

leaving Portsmouth at 18.30 with the return from Cherbourg at 23.59, would also be operated at weekends during the peak season.

The vessel earmarked to open the new operation was *Viking I*, which was duly renamed *Viking Victory* after Nelson's famous flagship which lies nearby to the ferry port at Portsmouth Dockyard. The Chairman of Townsend Thoresen, Keith Wickenden, said at the time that the decision to rename the ship had been made as a gesture to the people of Portsmouth who had welcomed them so warmly into their city.

The *Viking Venturer* and *Viking Valiant*, continued to operate to Le Havre and Cherbourg from Southampton; they did not transfer to Portsmouth until 1977.

Meanwhile, another ferry company in the Western Channel was rapidly expanding its operations from their humble beginnings of initially operating a freight service between Roscoff and Plymouth. Brittany Ferries, who had established a freight-only service in January 1973, were now rapidly expanding their operations, and like Townsend Thoresen they decided to use the new ferry terminal at Portsmouth to establish a new ferry service to St.Malo, using their newly acquired vessel *Armorique*.

In 1976 only the *Armorique* and *Viking Victory* were using the small ferry terminal of Portsmouth. Today the terminal operates up to thirty sailings during the peak summer season and also handles some of the largest ferries operating out of the British Isles.

TOWNSEND
THORESEN

The ***Viking Venturer*** pictured in the Solent prior to entering service between Southampton and Le Havre. *(Ferry Publications Library)*

EXPANSION OF PORTSMOUTH

1977-1982

To make greater utilisation of their fleet, Townsend Thoresen decided to transfer part of their Le Havre operation to Portsmouth in 1977. On 28th May, the *Viking Valiant* departed from Le Havre at 09.00 hours, and arrived at Portsmouth for the first time, enabling her to sail back to the French port at 14.30, ready for the night sailing to Southampton. The early morning sailing to Portsmouth and lunchtime sailing back to Le Havre, allowed the company to do an additional sailing a day. The experiment proved a great success, and from 1978 the operations were gradually scaled down at Southampton in favour of Portsmouth.

It was another success story for Townsend Thoresen, which culminated at the end of 1983 with the Company withdrawing their passenger operations from Southampton for the final time. Freight sailings continued at Southampton for a further twelve months until 30th December 1984, when the *Viking Trader* made the last sailing from the port.

P&O Normandy Ferries continued to soldier on with the *Dragon* and *Leopard*, offering a midday and midnight sailing from both Southampton and Le Havre. Both vessels were to prove very reliable, but by now they were now beginning to show their age compared with the superior vessels operated by Townsend Thoresen from Portsmouth. The company continued to lose its market share on the Le Havre service and eventually was to be taken over

The ***Armorique*** heads away from the Isle of Wight on her nine hour crossing between Portsmouth and St.Malo. *(FotoFlite)*

by Townsend Thoresen.

Following the transfer of Townsend Thoresen to Portsmouth, the *Viking Venturer* and *Viking Valiant* were employed on the Le Havre service, with the *Viking Victory* maintaining the Cherbourg service ,with additional summer support during the peak seasons from *Free Enterprise II*, *Free Enterprise III* and later *Free Enterprise V*.

Brittany Ferries' operations to St.Malo from Portsmouth were to prove an overwhelming success. Despite operational and technical difficulties during the first season, involving the withdrawal of the *Armorique* and charter of other vessels to substitute the operation, the Company attracted some 75,000 passengers and 18,000 cars in the first four months. In 1977, the *Armorique* was joined by the *Penn-ar-Bed* to offer increased capacity on the nine hour link. In 1978, the *Armorique* was replaced by the larger vessel *Prince of Brittany*, which was initally chartered for two years, before the

brittany ferries

Company bought her. The attractive looking vessel was to maintain the service until December 1988, when she was transferred to another route.

Sealink, the shipping division of British Rail, decided in 1977 that they would also transfer some of their operations to of Portsmouth from Weymouth. Ironically, the Company purchased one of the former Thoresen vessels from Townsend Thoresen to open the new operation from Portsmouth. The *Viking II* was purchased by British Rail in December 1976 for the new Portsmouth-Channel Islands service. Due to delays with the new ferry, the *Earl Godwin* was used to inaugurate the link on 8th November 1977. Some two months later on 16th January 1978 the former Thoresen vessel, now renamed *Earl William*, took up

A sunny August day in 1990-the ***Earl William*** is seen here leaving St.Helier, Jersey *(John Hendy)*

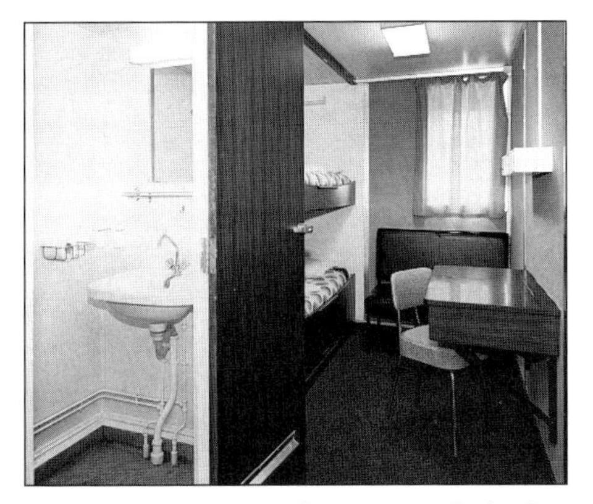

Left: A 2-berth cabin - ***Armorique***. Right: *Lounge bar -* **Penn-ar-Bed**. *(Ferry Publications Library)*

the route. She remained on the link for the next three years until being replaced by the larger *Earl Granville* (ex *Viking 4*).

Operations to both France and the Channel Islands continued to expand in the seventies and early eighties. By now the port was becoming heavily congested, especially during the morning and evening periods when ships departed and arrived at Pompey. For example, in 1980, Townsend Thoresen had departures from Portsmouth to Cherbourg at 08.30, 14.00, 19.30 and 23.59 to Le Havre at 15.00 hours Brittany Ferries to St.Malo at 08.30 and 22.00 hours and Sealink at 23.00 hours to the Channel Islands. Arrivals at the port included those

Brittany Ferries first purpose-built ship, the ***Penn-ar-Bed.*** *(FotoFlite)*

The ***Viking III*** pictured in the Solent in her original Thoresen Car Ferries livery inward bound to Southampton. *(FotoFlite)*

from Cherbourg 06.30, 12.30, 17.30 and 22.00 hours from Le Havre, 13.00 from St.Malo at 06.30 and 18.30, and from the Channel Islands 18.15. Over the next five years the growth of operations was to increase even more in the light of rising demand from the holiday trade and freight operators.

Ferry operations for the most time ran smoothly; however, in 1980 the ferry companies had to contend with the French fishermen's blockade of the Channel ports.

The ***Prince of Brittany*** was chartered in 1978 as a replacement to the ***Armorique*** on the St.Malo-Portsmouth service. *(Ferry Publications Library)*

Townsend Thoresen at Southampton and Portsmouth had their sailings very badly affected at the height of the holiday season. The *Viking Valiant* spent twenty-three hours at sea trying to get into the French port at Le Havre and the *Viking Venturer* twenty-six hours, after having to return following failure to get into Cherbourg first and then St.Malo. The *Viking Victory* was to take even longer than the 'Super Vikings', when she spent fifty-six hours at sea before getting back to Portsmouth without unloading. The *Free Enterprise II*, which was serving on the Portsmouth-Cherbourg link, finally beat the French fishermen's blockade with the sounds of 'Land of Hope and Glory' blaring over the ship's tannoy, on Sunday 17th August, when she was able to break the blockade of trawlers at the entrance to the terminal at Cherbourg and finally tied up with the aid of the frustrated motorists who drove off dockers and fishermen from the quayside. The fishermen were incensed by this and insisted that Captain Mike Edward return home by aeroplane. The company received the largest mailbag for years and adopted the slogan "It's the fleet you can't beat". The *Viking Venturer* and *Viking Valiant* later broke the blockade at Le Havre in the dead of night whilst the fishermen were caught off their guard.

Brittany Ferries were also faced with problems with their operations during the fishermen's industrial action. Trouble for them started on 13th August, when the first of the Channel ports were affected by the blockade, and some seven days later all the French ferry ports were closed by industrial action. Brittany Ferries were forced to use their Spanish port of Santander, and on 20th August, at intervals of some ninety minutes, three of their vessels sailed from Plymouth to Spain, taking stranded holiday makers on the twenty-three hour trip. The industrial action was to put the company to a lot of extra expense, as it not only closed the company's port, but also meant that the crews of the French ships were unable to

The ***Viking Valiant*** pictured arriving at Cherbourg from Portsmouth with the ***Queen Elizabeth 2*** in the background prior to her departure to New York. *(Ferry Publications Library)*

The ***Viking Venturer*** and ***Free Enterprise V*** seen passing each other in the English Channel. *(Ferry Publications Library)*

change over during the industrial action. On 21st August, the *Cornouailles* finally broke the blockade at Roscoff, and by the end of the week all the dramas were over as the French fishermen agreed to reopen the blockaded ports.

Two further ships of Otto Thoresen's original fleet were sold. Firstly, in late summer 1981, the *Viking IV* was sold to Philippinen interests and renamed *Guernsey*

The ***Europic Ferry*** replaced the smaller ***Viking IV*** on the Southampton-Le Havre freight service in 1981. *(Ferry Publications Library)*

Express. Her place on the Southampton freight service was taken by the older but larger *Europic Ferry*.

In early spring 1982 the Falklands War broke out, which provided major problems for Townsend Thoresen with three ships being requisitioned for the task force. The *Free Enterprise V*, which was going to replace the *Viking Victory* on the Cherbourg link in 1983, was brought into service early on the Southampton-Le Havre freight run in early April, prior to the departure of the *Europic Ferry* for the South Atlantic. The former Dover vessel was rostered to leave Southampton at 07.00 and return from Le Havre at 23.00. The *Free Enterprise V* was later switched to the Cherbourg link as from 20th May, prior to the arrival of the *Gaelic Ferry* being released from Felixstowe. Townsend Thoresen were forced to use one of the 'Super Vikings' on the freight run to Le Havre, leaving *Free Enterprise III*

alongside the other 'Super Viking' on the passenger service. To add to the troubles of the company during this period, while the *Free Enterprise III* was inward bound from Cherbourg to Southampton on 10th May, there was an engine-room explosion on board. The ship eventually resumed its power and arrived with 310 passengers on board at Southampton some twenty-one and half hours later. After some deliberation by the company because of the age of the ferry, it was decided to carry out repairs to the damaged ship.

With *Free Enterprise III* out of action, one of the 'Super Vikings' had to be transferred to the Cherbourg link, which in turn meant that the *Free Enterprise V* was left to handle

Following the success of the ***Earl William*** on the Portsmouth-Channel Islands service, the larger ***Earl Granville*** was purchased by Sealink to offer greater capacity as from March 1981. *(FotoFlite)*

all freight operations until the *Gaelic Ferry* arrived from Suffolk. The *Europic Ferry* returned from the Falklands on 17th July after a heroic time in the South Atlantic under the command of Captain Chris Clarke. After an extensive refit, she entered service once again on the Le Havre freight service on 26th August.

The *Viking III* was sold during 1982 to Norwegian interests, and some six months later the *Viking Victory* was sold to Cypriot interests. All four original Thoresen Vikings had now been sold. It is interesting to note that all four vessels still remain in service in very much their original guise.

1983-1986

In 1983, Brittany Ferries, which had been formed to transport farm produce from Brittany to England, celebrated its tenth birthday, boasting a fleet of six ships and four ferry routes (St.Malo-Portsmouth, Roscoff-Plymouth, Plymouth-Santander and Roscoff-Cork). The next ten years of growth of the company was to be even more dramatic. In 1984, Brittany Ferries in partnership with Huelin Renouf and the haulage company MMD, set up a consortium to start a rival ferry service to that of Sealink between the Channel Islands and Britain. The company chose Portsmouth as their port to operate the new operation using the *Benodet* (chartered to Brittany Ferries for their

The ***Earl William*** undergoing her extensive refit in Denmark prior to her opening the **Starliner** and **Bateaux De Luxe** service in 1984. *(Ferry Publications Library)*

Above: The ***Earl Granville*** seen arriving at Portsmouth sporting Sealink British Ferries livery in June 1984. *(Miles Cowsill)*

Below: The ***Corbière*** pictured on her morning sailing to the Channel Islands from Portsmouth in June 1984. *(Richard Kirkman)*

CHANNEL ISLAND FERRIES

Roscoff route in 1983). The new service started on Thursday, 28th March 1985 with the former Brittany Ferries ship renamed *Corbière*. The new operation branded as Channel Island Ferries was to prove an overnight success, and by mid-summer the company was claiming that it had captured 85% of the passenger traffic to Jersey and Guernsey from Portsmouth. In July the new company were taking delivery of the third reprint of their brochure.

In the light of the new service a new-style ferry service to the Channel Islands was started by Sealink, now a privatised company purchased by the American controlled company Sea Containers Ltd and branded now as Sealink British Ferries. The new style company decided to offer an up-market ferry service to the Islands under the banner of 'Starliner' and 'Bateaux de Luxe' route. The *Earl William* and *Earl Granville* were sent to Denmark for a £5 million refit to provide luxury accommodation for just 400 passengers each on the new style Portsmouth-Channel Islands service. The 'William' was first to arrive back at Portsmouth from her major refit on the morning of 23rd April 1985. She duly entered service the next day, followed by the *Earl Granville* some six days later.

The new Sealink operation allowed for nightly departures from Portsmouth direct to the Channel Islands and an inward sailing from the Islands direct to Portsmouth. The daylight sailings to and from the islands offered a slightly longer passage with calls at Cherbourg. The calls at Cherbourg allowed the company to establish a new link to the Islands from France for car and passenger traffic.

Whilst both ferries were luxuriously

Strike-bound fleet of Sealink British Ferries in October 1985. Left to right, the ***Earl William***, ***Earl Harold*** and ***Earl Godwin***. *(Ferry Publications Library)*

Above: The ***Earl William*** sporting British Ferries livery at St.Peter Port in May 1985. *(Miles Cowsill)*
Below: Channel Island Ferries ***Corbière*** captured 85% of the passenger traffic between Portsmouth and the Channel Islands during her first season in operation in 1984. *(Miles Cowsill)*

appointed, the fare structure which accompanied them was not conducive to passengers, compared with that of Channel Island Ferries or that of the airlines. At the end of the first season, Sealink were faced with mounting losses from the new service, and were forced the following year to introduce a new fare structure in an effort to see off Channel Island Ferries' success of the previous season.

The level of traffic on the Channel Island Ferries operation for 1986 was slightly reduced following Sealink's reorganisation of their fares and sailings to the Islands. However, Channel Island Ferries managed to capture 55% of the traffic from Portsmouth.

During late summer, Channel Island Ferries and Sealink British Ferries entered private talks about merging their operations, in an effort to save money and reduce an over-capacity between Portsmouth and the Channel Islands. Following these talks a joint statement was made on 30th September. Channel Island Ferries and Sealink British Ferries announced that they would join forces on the Channel Island services and the new operation would be called British Channel Island Ferries (BCIF).

As a result of this announcement with the inevitable reduction of vessels serving the Islands and redundancies, officers and crews of the four Sealink Channel Island vessels immediately took industrial action. A series of sit-ins began on board the four ships, the *Earl William* at St.Peter Port, the *Earl Godwin* at Weymouth, the *Earl Granville* at Cherbourg, and later the *Earl Harold* when she arrived at Portsmouth. The islands having been served by five ferries during the summer were now left in the hands of one vessel - the *Corbière*. She was able to cope with the autumn passenger traffic, but freight soon began to pile up on the quayside on the Islands and in Britain.

Meanwhile at Guernsey, the *Earl William* had blocked the linkspan at St.Peter Port, preventing the *Corbière* from docking, so Channel Island Ferries decided that they would have to unload cars and freight at St.Helier. Traffic for Guernsey was then transferred to Torbay Seaways *Devoniun*, which had a side-loading ramp and did not have to use the linkspan. Eventually, the *Earl William* did move from the linkspan following agreement being reached with the crew of the ship to allow the *Corbière* to dock once again at the port. The 'William' then sailed to Weymouth to join the rest of the Sealink fleet now on strike.

In the event Sealink British Ferries were unable to reach agreement with the NUS and Officers Union to join the new venture, and as a result of this they were unable to offer the *Earl Granville* and the *Earl Harold* (for Weymouth) for the new operation.

Channel Island Ferries then took out a series of court injunctions against their new partners, which they won. Under the interim agreement with Sealink, Channel Island Ferries were allowed to trade as BCIF. Sealink also undertook not to offer any services to the Islands for the next twelve months.

Following the joint venture falling through, BCIF quickly had to charter two vessels, to maintain a credible service for the forthcoming summer season and to move freight between the mainland and the Islands. BCIF looked to Brittany Ferries for a freight ship and chartered the *Breizh-Izel*. The vessel ran opposite the *Corbière* between Portsmouth and the Channel Islands.

Eventually a suitable vessel was found to operate the Weymouth route, which the Company had to maintain following the demise of Sealink's operations from the port. A chartered Greek ship by the name of *Baroness M* (ex *Lion*), which had been in the

The French registered ***Leopard*** inward bound from Southampton to Le Havre. *(FotoFlite)*

ownership of Normandy Ferries.

In December 1984, Townsend Thoresen announced that the two 'Super Vikings' serving at Portsmouth, the *Viking Venturer* and *Viking Valiant*, together with two of the 'Free Enterprise' class ships at Dover, would be enlarged to meet the increasing demands for freight space on the Le Havre service. The

Townsend Thoresen's freight vessel ***Viking Trader*** seen here arriving at Portsmouth from Le Havre. *(Miles Cowsill)*

The ***Viking Venturer*** captured mid-Channel en route to Le Havre. In the background, ***Free Enterprise V*** can be seen inward bound to Portsmouth from Cherbourg. *(Ferry Publications Library)*

Above: The elegant ***Duc de Normandie*** outward bound from Portsmouth to Caen. *(Miles Cowsill)*
Below: The ***Europic Ferry*** at Southampton following her arrival back from the Falklands on 17th July 1982. *(David Marshall)*

two 'Super Vikings' would be fitted with a larger forward section as well as being horizontally cut in two with an additional full length vehicle deck inserted, enabling both vessels to carry an additional sixty lorries. The conversion of both ships would take an eight/nine months period during the winter of 1985/86.

Meanwhile, on the 3rd December 1984, P&O Ferries announced that they would be moving their operations from Southampton to Portsmouth, a move which was prompted by yet another period of industrial unrest at the port. On New Year's Day, the *Lion* was moved from Dover to the Le Havre link to cover for the refits of the *Leopard* and *Dragon*. The next day, P&O announced that they had sold all their interests on the English Channel to Townsend Thoresen for £12.5 million. The merger of P&O Normandy Ferries and TTF solved one of the problems at Portsmouth for the pending summer season, as *Free Enterprise V* would not be available for the Cherbourg route as she was required on the Dover-Zeebrugge link, while *Free Enterprise VI* and *VII* underwent their jumboisation.

Normandy Ferries

P&O Ferries

The ex P&O ship *Dragon*, and the French registered *Leopard* were quickly brought under Townsend Thoresen management and were included in the schedules for the Company at Portsmouth for the forthcoming season. During summer, they covered all the Le Havre sailings with the chartered roll-on/roll-off freighters *Viking Trader* and *Stena Sailer*, while the *Viking Venturer* and *Viking Valiant* covered the Cherbourg route. The *Dragon*, and the *Leopard's* passenger areas were upgraded for their new role and improvements were made to their engines to enable the vessels to maintain their three sailings a day required between Portsmouth and Le Havre. Following the *Lion* covering for the refits, she was sold by the Company to Greek interests, eventually returning to Britain some two years later on charter to BCIF as the *Portelet*.

In October 1985, Townsend Thoresen

TOWNSEND THORESEN
Fleet development programme

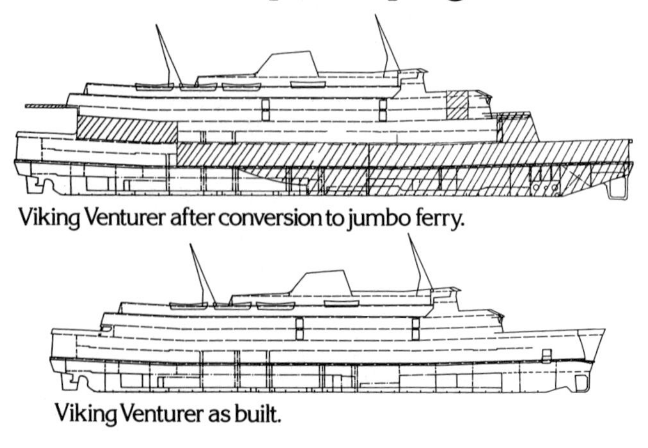

Viking Venturer after conversion to jumbo ferry.

Viking Venturer as built.

The **Duc de Normandie** arrives at Portsmouth on her inaugural voyage from Caen, escorted by two naval tugs. *(Ferry Publications Library)*

decided to convert two of their freight ships at Felixstowe to multi-purpose passenger/freight ships for their Zeebrugge route at a cost of £9 million each. The conversion of these ships would release the *Viking Voyager* and *Viking Viscount* (sisters to the 'Super Vikings' at Portsmouth) so that they could be transferred to the Portsmouth-Cherbourg route. On their arrival, the *Dragon* would be transferred to Cairnryan, while the *Leopard* would be sold.

Meanwhile, in 1985, Brittany Ferries announced that they had been investigating for some time a new link from Portsmouth to Normandy, following the decision by their rivals at Portsmouth, Townsend Thoresen, not to open a new ferry service between the port of Ouistreham (north of Caen) and Portsmouth. Brittany Ferries were offered the new French port instead. The company could see the new terminal offered great potential and would enable them to rival the operations of Townsend Thoresen at Cherbourg and Le Havre. The new link from Normandy would operate from a new berth and terminal on the seaward side of the entrance to the canal serving Caen. The *Prinses Beatrix* (9,367 gross tonnes) was purchased for the new route from SMZ in Holland. She would be not only the biggest ship of the fleet, but also the largest ferry ever to operate out of Portsmouth.

The *Prinses Beatrix* underwent a major refit in the Netherlands prior to entering service with Brittany Ferries. A number of names with a Normandy feel to them were considered for the vessel, including *William the Conqueror*; in the event she was named *Duc de Normandie*. The French design company AIA were appointed by Brittany Ferries to redesign the interior areas of the ship. The aim was to give passengers a taste of France as soon as they boarded the ship. The main passenger lounge was named after the French artist Claude Monet, who lived in Normandy in a little village called Giverny. The main bar was to boast a Calvados still, whilst the adjoining wine bar featured a Norman cider press. The new ship also offered a patisserie.

Prior to the new car service opening on 6th June 1986, the *Armorique* made two special round trips between Portsmouth and the city of Caen to launch the new operation.

The *Duc de Normandie* entered service on 5th June 1986 on the 23.30 sailing to Normandy. Her extremely well appointed accommodation brought a new sense of style and taste in ferry travel from the port, setting new standards on the Channel and in turn offering a real challenge to the other rival ferry operators.

With early encouraging signs of bookings

Above: The ***Viking Venturer*** makes a fine sight as she leaves Portsmouth Harbour en route to Cherbourg in June 1985 prior to her jumboisation. *(Miles Cowsill)*
Below: The ***Venture***r seen here on sea trials in June 1986 following her jumboisation in Germany. *(FotoFlite)*

Above: The ***Europic Ferry*** inward bound to Portsmouth from Le Havre in August 1982 following her extensive refit after serving in the Falklands War. *(Miles Cowsill)*
Below: The former P&O Normandy Ferries vessel ***Dragon*** pictured here arriving at Portsmouth in June 1985 in Townsend Thoresen livery. *(Miles Cowsill)*

and good freight loadings, ahead of expectations, Brittany Ferries started to consider plans for jumboising the *Duc de Normandie* to meet the expected demands for the forthcoming season. One of the plans considered for the vessel was cutting the ship horizontally in two, giving her a new upper car deck. In the event none of these plans went ahead.

Following the decision not to jumboise the *Duc de Normandie* or to carry out similar work to the *Quiberon*, Brittany Ferries invited tenders to build a new purpose-built ferry for their Santander route to meet the growing summer demand on this ferry link which was now ten years old. A French yard was appointed to build the new ship, which entered service as the *Bretagne* in July 1989.

On the 20th January 1986, the governments of France and Britain announced firm details for a fixed link across the Channel.

Meanwhile, the new hull sections for Townsend Thoresen's *Viking Valiant* and *Viking Venturer*, were launched as one unit end to end in Germany. Work started on the *Viking Venturer* in December 1985, and during the weekend of 4th/5th January the first section of her super-structure was lifted from her existing hull in sub-zero conditions, which made the work extremely difficult. Unlike the 'Free Enterprise' twins, the super-structure of the 'Super Viking' class had to be lifted in two operations as their passenger accommodation was much larger. The delicate lifting of the aft section of the *Viking Venturer* took some four hours. The forward section was then removed and left with the aft section on the quay ready for the next part of the operation. An extra car deck was constructed after the forward bow section had been removed. The new bow section was then joined to the existing hull of the 'Venturer'. After the hull had been joined together the super-structure was then placed on the joined hull sections.

During the conversion of the 'Venturer', an industrial dispute occurred within the Townsend Thoresen fleet, and the Company were forced to do some quick thinking to prevent delay of the jumboisation of the *Viking Valiant*. The 'Valiant' was sent to Bremerhaven in February so she was not caught up in any possible strikes.

During March, Townsend Thoresen announced that the *Leopard* would be withdrawn from service with the loss of 140 French seamen's jobs as a result of the disposal of this ship. The linkspan at Le Havre was immediately blocked by the French crew of the *Leopard*, as a result of which all services from Portsmouth were diverted to Cherbourg. Meanwhile, the transfers of the first of the 'Super Vikings' from Felixstowe were

The aft section of the passenger accommodation of ***Viking Venturer*** is slowly lifted in sub-zero conditions. *(Ferry Publications Library)*

The ***Earl Godwin*** operated on the Portsmouth-Cherbourg route during 1988 with the ***Earl Granville***. *(Maritime Photographic)*

delayed due to industrial action at the Suffolk port.

Eventually Townsend Thoresen agreed that the *Leopard's* crew would be transferred to the *Viking Viscount* until the end of September 1986. It was also agreed that the 'Viscount' should be transferred to the French flag, but due to pressure from the British crew at Portsmouth to allow the first 'Super Viking' from Suffolk to remain under the British flag, it was the 'Voyager' which was re-registered at Le Havre. The French Seamen's Union agreed that they would stand down from the *Viking Voyager* on 1st October and accept redundancy terms, as long as the freighter *Viking Trader* was also withdrawn from the Le Havre route.

The *Viking Viscount* entered service at Portsmouth on the Le Havre run on 7th May and was joined by the *Viking Voyager* on 22nd May on the Cherbourg link. The 'Voyager' was re-registered under the French flag on 27th May.

While the industrial unrest was going on at Le Havre, work was also stopped on the new double-deck ramp, and building work at Portsmouth also got behind. The *Viking Venturer* underwent sea trials following her jumboisation on 6th May and sailed to Portsmouth some seven days later. After a brief call at Portsmouth, she then sailed to Southampton for further work to her passenger accommodation and on 19th May she entered operations.

The *Viking Venturer* now looked a very different ship and rather dwarfed her newly arrived sisters from Felixstowe. Sadly the conversion spoilt the former good looks of the ship with an extra deck and conversion of the bow section. Neither of the new linkspans at Portsmouth and Le Havre were completed until July, so the *Viking Venturer* was put on the Cherbourg route until the arrival of her other jumboised sister from Germany. The 'Valiant' entered service on 3rd July on the 23.30 sailing to Le Havre; meanwhile the 'Venturer' slotted in a week earlier on the Le Havre operation on the completion of both linkspans at Le Havre and Portsmouth.

The French registered *Leopard* was sold in July to Cypriot interests and renamed *Countess M*. Meanwhile the *Dragon*, following a refit in Scotland, entered service on the Cairnryan-Larne service on the 8th July, and was renamed *Ionic Ferry*.

The *Viking Viscount* completed her season on the Cherbourg service on the 7th September, and following a number of day-trip charters, was sent to lay up for the winter. Meanwhile, the *Viking Voyager* continued the winter schedules for the Cherbourg route, and on 1st October was transferred back to the British flag. The *Viking Trader* was withdrawn from service in October, as agreed with the French unions. She subsequently returned to the Le Havre operation the next season before being sold to Pandoro, the next autumn.

On 5th December 1986, Townsend Thoresen (European Ferries Group) was taken over by the P&O Group. The impact of the takeover was to see, some ten months later, the demise of the famous brand name of Townsend Thoresen. The vessels appeared the next summer with their orange hulls, inspired by Thoresen Car Ferries, but with pale blue funnels, and the TT logo was removed in favour of the famous P&O house flag.

1987-1991

During the late summer it was disclosed by the P&O Group that the house name of Townsend Thoresen would disappear as from 21st October 1987, as part of their reorganisation of the ferry company. In future the company would trade as P&O European Ferries. On the evening of 21st October, the *Viking Venturer* and the *Viking Valiant* set sail from Portsmouth and Le Havre. The TT house flag was run down from the main mast for the last time.

The vessels appeared as from 1988 in the new P&O Ferries livery of dark blue hulls and funnels incorporating the house flag on the twin funnels of the 'Super Vikings'.

Just before the end of 1987, Brittany Ferries announced that they planned to introduce a second vessel on their Caen service during the next season, as from 19th May to 11th September 1988, with the *Duc de Normandie*. The company took a one-year bare boat charter of the Yugoslavian, built ship *Gotland*, which would be able to accommodate 1,200 passengers. She was

Townsend Thoresen Logo.

The ***Viking Voyager*** inward from Cherbourg in June 1986 under the French flag. *(Miles Cowsill)*

Above: The former ***Prince of Brittany*** was renamed ***Reine Mathilde*** following her transfer to the Caen-Portsmouth route in February 1989. *(Ferry Publications Library)*
Below: The ***Duc de Normandie*** and ***Viking Venturer*** are seen here at Portsmouth Continental Ferry Port pending their early morning departures to France. *(Richard Kirkman)*

not due to enter service until May 1988, but due to major industrial action throughout the fleets of P&O European Ferries and Sealink, the Swedish flag vessel was brought into service early although initially only to convey school parties and freight between Caen and Portsmouth. The situation at Portsmouth became so serious with a backlog of passenger and freight traffic that Brittany Ferries were forced to reorganise their schedules and operations to meet the increased demand brought on by the strikes. The *Armorique* was brought into service early to cover the St.Malo route, releasing the *Prince of Brittany* to transfer to the Caen service to operate additional passenger sailings with the *Duc de Normandie* and *Gotland*. A record for ships operating on the link was set in the late spring, when the *Breizh-Izel* was also brought into service, making a total of four ships on the six-hour route at one time. Once the industrial action which had plagued the British operators had been resolved, the Caen link returned to a two ship passenger operation. During the summer, the freight ship *Gabriele Wehr* was also chartered to support the passenger vessels on the Caen service.

Meanwhile, in June, Brittany Ferries announced that they had purchased the B&I ferry *Connacht* for delivery in the autumn. The newly acquired ship had originally been built for the Irish company in 1978 for the now defunct Cork-Pembroke Dock route. It was disclosed by Brittany Ferries that she would undergo a £2 million refit prior to her becoming the principal ship on the St.Malo route as from 1989, in place of the *Prince of Brittany*, along with the *Armorique*. This would allow the *Prince of Brittany* to be transferred to support the *Duc de Normandie* on the Caen service, to offer three sailings a day from each port.

The *Tregastel* was transferred in the autumn from Roscoff to the Caen-Portsmouth service to support the *Duc de Normandie* for the winter. The original winter schedule had allowed for a single round trip between Caen and Portsmouth, but with the route's booming freight traffic put at 30% above the same period of 1987, the company decided to increase the schedules.

The Swedish registered ***Gotland*** was chartered by Brittany Ferries in 1988 to offer additional capacity on the Caen-Portsmouth service with the ***Duc de Normandie***. *(Maritime Photographic)*

The *Duc de Normandie* was joined by the former *Prince of Brittany*, which for her new role was renamed *Reine Mathilde*, after William the Conqueror's queen. Following her extensive refit, she made her passenger debut on the route on 17th March. In addition to extra passenger sailings offered for 1989, further capacity was provided by the newly chartered Truckline vessel *Normandie Shipper* on this link.

Brittany Ferries were to have a record year in 1989, with some 2.1 million passengers travelling on their six-route network. On the back of this success, in May 1990, Brittany Ferries announced plans to build two new vessels to replace some of the older tonnage in the fleet and to expand the Caen-Portsmouth operations. The contract for the first ferry, a new jumbo ship for the Caen service, was awarded to Masa Yard at Helsinki in Finland. A second ship for the Truckline passenger operation (Cherbourg-Poole) was later secured with Masa. Both orders were worth some £130 million, and each vessel was to take two years to build and would be built to the new 1990 SOLAS specifications, with designs reflecting the latest international thinking on safety at sea.

The first of the new vessels being built in Finland, the *Barfleur*, for the Cherbourg-Poole service, took to the water on 26th July 1991. Work on the larger vessel for the Caen service, to be named *Normandie*, continued for delivery in June 1992. Brittany Ferries also announced later in the year that the *Duc de Normandie* would undergo an extensive £3 million refit and upgrading of her passenger accommodation, prior to the *Normandie* entering service with her the next year. At Portsmouth, it was announced by the City Council that work would start on the construction of a new double-deck linkspan and extended berth for the new superferry to operate on the Caen link. Meanwhile, the Chamber of Commerce at Caen announced that they would undertake similar work to that of Portsmouth.

On 19th August 1988, British Channel Island Ferries announced that as from 2nd

In September 1988, the Isle of Man Steam Packet vessel ***Mona's Queen*** was chartered by the French Post Office to support their **La Poste** at the start of the Round the World Yacht Race. The elegant vessel is seen here leaving Portsmouth for Cherbourg on 2nd September 1989. *(John Hendy)*

Above: The ***Pride of Bilbao*** makes an impressive view as she leaves 'Pompey' en route to Bilbao. *(Maritime Photographic)*
Below: The ***Duchesse Anne*** appeared on the St.Malo-Portsmouth route with Brittany Ferries as from February 1989. The vessel is seen here swinging off St.Malo on her nine-hour passage to Portsmouth. *(Miles Cowsill)*

January 1989 they would move both their passenger and freight operations from Portsmouth to Poole. The new mainland terminal would offer faster crossings of up to two hours on some sailings. A month later, BCIF secured long-term charter of the *Scirocco* (8,987 gross tonnes) from Cenargo Navigation Limited. She would replace the *Corbière* in the New Year and would be the largest ship ever to operate between Britain and the Channel Islands. She was renamed *Rozel* after the north-east bay in Jersey, and was able to carry 300 cars and 1,300 passengers. The acquisition of the new vessel by BCIF allowed the *Corbière* to return to Brittany Ferries to operate on their Cherbourg-Poole service with the *Tregastel*. The *Corbière* undertook her last sailing from Portsmouth to the Channel Islands on 31st December 1988. On her return to Portsmouth on 2nd January 1989, she sailed light to Poole before undertaking the inaugural sailing from the Dorset port to Guernsey and Jersey.

The move of BCIF from Portsmouth to Poole was not greeted by everyone as a positive move. Freight operators especially did not like the port of Poole and pressure from them led to Mainland Marketing Delivery in conjunction with Commodore Shipping starting their own freight service between 'Pompey' and the Islands. Sealink's *Earl Godwin* was initially used by MMD and Commodore until they were able to charter a suitable freight vessel which they renamed *Pride of Portsmouth*.

Sealink British Ferries resumed sailings at Portsmouth again in 1988, offering initially a one-ship operation as from 30th March between Portsmouth and Cherbourg with a Saturday and Tuesday sailing to Guernsey. The *Earl Godwin* joined the *Earl Granville* as from the 15th July, offering additional services between Portsmouth and Cherbourg. A similar service was offered the next season by Sealink, using the *Earl*

Hoverspeed Great Britain seen arriving at Portsmouth during her rather erratic season on the Western Channel in 1990. *(Maritime Photographic)*

P&O European Ferries

Granville only as the *Earl Godwin* was transferred to the Weymouth-Cherbourg link.

The *Earl Granville* hit national headlines when unfortunately she hit a series of rocks outside Cherbourg Harbour on the morning of 19th August 1989. A 15-metre gash in the hull ruptured all the tanks of the vessel, allowing seawater into her fuel tanks and then around her engines. Some 700 people were on board the ship when the incident occurred. She did eventually make port and was able to discharge, and was then withdrawn from service for major repairs. No other ship was available at the time within the Sealink fleet to take her place. The service was suspended for fifteen days until the Isle of Man Steam Packet vessel *Mona's Queen* became available after being chartered by a French concern to follow the French yacht *La Poste* at the start of the Round the World Yacht Race in the Solent on 2nd September. The *Mona's Queen* took up the Portsmouth-Cherbourg route on 4th September for ten days until a more suitable and larger vessel could be chartered. Irish Ferries' *Saint Patrick II* arrived at Portsmouth on the morning of 15th September to maintain the operation of Sealink between Portsmouth-Cherbourg and Guernsey for the rest of the season. The *Saint Patrick II* was to make headlines in Guernsey when she first docked at the port, being the largest ferry ever to dock at St.Peter Port Harbour.

In May 1989, the Cherbourg and Le Havre services of P&O European Ferries celebrated their first twenty-five years.

The ***Commodore Clipper*** pictured in the evening sun arriving at 'Pompey' from Guernsey. *(Miles Cowsill)*

The ***Pride of Cherbourg*** and ***Pride of Winchester*** pass each other off the Isle of Wight. *(FotoFlite)*

Special celebrations were held by P&O European Ferries to celebrate the success of both routes. Meanwhile, as part of a reorganisation of the former trading company, Townsend Thoresen, P&O European Ferries renamed all their vessels at Portsmouth. The *Viking Venturer* became the *Pride of Hampshire*, with her jumboised sister *Viking Valiant* being renamed *Pride of Le Havre*. The former Felixstowe vessels, *Viking Voyager* and *Viking Viscount*, became the *Pride of Cherbourg* and *Pride of Winchester* respectively.

A fast ferry service between Portsmouth and Cherbourg was announced by Hoverspeed in early 1990, using a new craft currently under construction in Tasmania. The fast ferry service would initially operate three round sailings a day, but these sailings would be increased during August to five crossings taking some two and a half hours only, compared to that of the conventional ferry of some four hours and fifteen minutes.

The new wave type catamaran hit world headlines on her delivery voyage when her owners Sea Containers decided to challenge for the Blue Ribbon Hales Trophy between America and Britain. *Hoverspeed Great Britain*, challenged for the trophy in June under the command of Captain John Lloyd making the crossing in 3 days, 7 hours and 54 minutes, cutting some three hours off the world record held by the liner *United States'* crossing of 1952.

The challenging crossing of the Atlantic by the *Hoverspeed Great Britain* stretched the craft's technical ability to its limits, and as a result the new fast ferry service from Portsmouth was delayed. *Hoverspeed Great*

Prior to the arrival of the ***Hoverspeed Great Britain***, the ***Earl Granville*** was used by Hoverspeed to maintain her Portsmouth-Cherbourg link. The vessel is seen here arriving early morning at Portsmouth. *(Maritime Photographic)*

Britain had been due to enter service during early July, but with technical difficulties and following inspections and insistence on certain modifications to the design of the craft by both British and French authorities, she was delayed from entering service until 14th August. In the meantime the company were forced to use an old favourite to Portsmouth, the *Earl Granville*, to maintain the new operation. Eventually the new revolutionary craft did enter operations on Tuesday, 14th August with the 08.30 sailing to Cherbourg. She had to come out of service again on 1st September for water jet adjustments, returning to service some ten days later. On 16th September the craft was withdrawn again for repairs, with work not being completed until 13th October. On 17th January 1991, Hoverspeed announced that they planned to withdraw their operations between Portsmouth and Cherbourg for at least a year, maybe two, until such time as operations on their Boulogne and Calais service had been resolved. *Hoverspeed Great Britain* completed her last sailing between Portsmouth and Cherbourg on 6th January. The SeaCat craft then sailed to refit at Cherbourg and transferred to Dover.

No ferry service was operated by Sealink British Ferries from Portsmouth in 1990. However, after a protracted hostile takeover bid, which James Sherwood, Chairman of Sea Containers Ltd. strongly resisted, April 1990 saw Sealink UK Limited become part of the Gothenburg-based Stena Line for £259 million. The lucrative Isle of Wight services and Hoverspeed were not included in the sale. The Sealink arm of operations was rebranded as Sealink Stena Line. As part of reorganisation of the company, Sealink Stena Line announced that they would open a new ferry service between Southampton and Cherbourg on 28th June 1991 using their vessel *St.Nicholas*, which would be renamed *Stena Normandy*.

During the peak season she would operate from Southampton on Tuesday, Friday and Sunday at 10.30 and 23.59 with inward sailings from Cherbourg at 18.30. On Mondays, Thursdays and Saturdays schedules from Southampton would be at 16.00, with sailings from Cherbourg at 09.30 and 23.59. On Wednesdays the vessel would only offer an 18.30 sailing from France and a 23.59 sailing from Southampton. From 23rd September, only one round sailing a day would be offered, apart from certain peak weekends.

The *Stena Normandy* undertook berthing trials at Southampton on the 20th January 1991, prior to returning to Harwich from refit. A new passenger terminal was provided at berth 30 at Southampton. The

service proved very popular during its first season and the next year the 'Normandy' was joined by a freight vessel *Stena Traveller*. The route was to carry in 1992 a total of 508,142 passengers and over 90,000 cars.

With the expansion of operations and new tonnage coming on stream at Brittany Ferries, P&O European Ferries began to look for new tonnage to replace their jumboised 'Super Vikings'. Very little suitable tonnage could be found by the company in the now thriving European

Sealink Stena Line re-established the Southampton-Cherbourg service in 1991 with the ***Stena Normandy***. This view shows the 'Normandy' passing the freight vessel ***Stena Traveller*** during 1992 when the Southampton-Cherbourg route was a two-vessel operation. *(Ferry Publications Library)*

ferry market. The folly of P&O Normandy Ferries in the seventies in failing to replace the *Dragon* and the *Leopard*, in the light of Townsend Thoresen's new tonnage at the time, was very much at the back of the British operators' minds.

Meanwhile, in anticipation of the arrival of the new superferry for Brittany Ferries, the *Normandie*, the *Duc de Normandie* was sent for her major overall in January 1992. The *Armorique* and the *Quiberon* were sent to cover the Caen service. On the return of the refurbishment of the 'Duc' in March, the *Armorique* remained on the link in a support role until the arrival of the *Normandie*. In April, Brittany Ferries took delivery of the first of their superferries, the *Barfleur* for the Cherbourg-Poole service. A month earlier, the company had announced that they had purchased the German ferry *Nils Holgersson* from TT Line for £70 million for their Spanish operation. The vessel would undergo a major building programme and overhaul to make her more suitable for the Spanish route. On her entry into service in 1993, the *Bretagne* would be transferred to the St.Malo-Portsmouth route, in place of the *Armorique* and *Duchesse Anne*.

Brittany Ferries

The ***Normandie*** leaves Portsmouth on her first commercial sailing to Caen.
(Maritime Photographic)

The elegant ***Bretagne*** pictured on 29th January 1993 on her inaugural sailing between Portsmouth and Santander. *(Maritime Photographic)*

1992-1995

On 14th June 1992, under the command of Captain Bertrand Apperry, the *Normandie* entered Portsmouth for the first time. The arrival of the vessel made her the largest ferry ever to operate from Pompey to date. On Monday, 16th June 1992, she entered commercial operations between Caen and Portsmouth. Her entry into operations increased the capacity on the route by some 40% overnight. Following the giant ferry slotting into the timetable, the *Armorique* was transferred to the St.Malo-Portsmouth service for what was going to be her last season on the route, prior to the arrival of the *Bretagne* on the link the following year. The *Normandie* was a far cry from the early days of the Breton company, boasting 220 luxury cabins and a capacity for 2,120 passengers and space for 630 cars on two decks. The elegant interior of the superferry was designed to cruise-like standards with the main accommodation situated over four decks. Her stylish passenger areas included two cinemas, a duty-free shopping mall, Le Derby bar, a self-service restaurant, the Deauville à la carte restaurant and terrace bar and the Pays d'Auge teashop with a most elegant reception area for passengers arriving on board. Original paintings by selected artists from Normandy graced the vessel's air conditioned interior. With an impressive length of 161 metres and a beam of 26 metres, she set new standards for the nineties on the English Channel, as had the *Duc de Normandie* in 1986, when she had opened the Caen link.

Eventually MMD's operations were

A crowded seafront at Portsmouth welcomes the ***Pride of Bilbao*** on her inaugural visit to the port. *(P&O European Ferries)*

brought under the wing of Commodore Ferries, a Guernsey based company. The *Pride of Portsmouth* was later renamed *Norman Commodore,* she was later rejoined by the chartered vessel *Commodore Clipper* as further support on the links to Guernsey and Jersey from Portsmouth.

On 29th January 1993, the *Bretagne* made her debut on the new seasonal ferry service between Portsmouth and Santander, which would operate until March and again from November through the winter. Meanwhile, during the same month, Brittany Ferries took delivery of the *Nils Holgersson* from TT Line. The German registered vessel was sent to Italy for an extensive overhaul and emerged as the *Val de Loire* later in the year.

The major investment, not only in new tonnage but in extensive staff training, was to pay handsome dividends for Brittany Ferries during 1992, when the AA awarded Brittany Ferries a five star rating for the *Normandie* and *Bretagne*, making it the only company to receive the highest accolade for ferries operating on the Channel.

The *Armorique* completed her summer spell on the St.Malo service on Wednesday, 30th September 1992. Five days later, ending her summer schedules, the vessel was chartered by British Steel to start the Round the World Yacht Race in the Solent. In the meantime the *Duchesse Anne* was left to maintain the St.Malo service until the 30th December. The *Duchesse Anne* had to be withdrawn from service for repairs following a collision with another ship at St.Malo, and the *Armorique* was brought back, completing her last commercial sailing with the company at the end of the year. The next season this graceful and popular ship was laid up at St.Malo as a reserve vessel in case of any mishaps to the rest of the fleet. The vessel never saw service again with Brittany Ferries and was later sold to Chinese interests.

In early January 1993, it was announced that P&O European Ferries had secured a three-year charter of Viking Line's *Olympia* to run a new ferry service from Portsmouth to Bilbao in Spain. The long-awaited new year round operation to Spain had been mooted by the company for some period of time, but no suitable vessel had been forthcoming in the charter market. The Swedish vessel offered an impressive range of public rooms, including three restaurants, conference rooms, cinema, saunas, swimming pool and solarium. The vehicle deck would be able to accommodate 600 cars on her thirty hour passage between the UK and Spain. The massive vessel, the world's tenth largest ferry, with berth accommodation for 2,447 passengers, would emerge as the *Pride of Bilbao* for the new link which she was to open in April. At 37,587 gross tonnes, she was to be the biggest ferry to have served a British port and is still to date the largest ferry ever to use Portsmouth.

The new service to Spain by P&O European Ferries went into direct competition with that of Brittany Ferries established service during the summer from Plymouth to Santander and their seasonal service in the winter from Portsmouth.

The *Pride of Bilbao* made her first appearance at Portsmouth on Sunday, 18th April with hundreds of sightseers crowding the shores of Portsmouth and Southsea to see the largest ferry ever to enter Portsmouth Harbour. Some ten days later, on the 28th April, the *Pride of Bilbao* made her maiden voyage to Spain.

At about the same time as the new ferry service opened, P&O European Ferries

The ***Pride of Bilbao*** slowly manoeuvres out of Portsmouth Harbour on her first sailing to Bilbao on 29th April 1993. *(Eric Brett)*

P&O European Ferries acquired the ***Olau Hollandia*** and ***Olau Britannia*** in March 1994 for their Portsmouth-Le Havre service. In this view the ***Olau Hollandia***, renamed ***Pride of Le Havre*** in May 1994, is seen leaving Sheerness. *(Ferry Publications Library)*

were hopeful that they had found suitable tonnage to replace the 'Super Vikings' on the Le Havre service. The company hoped to acquire from Viking Line, the same shipping company that they had chartered the *Pride of Bilbao* from, the *Athena* and *Kalypso*, as replacement vessels. In the event, the company were unsuccessful in securing both superferries.

With very few other vessels available, the company was forced to carry on with the existing tonnage, which was now beginning to show its age compared to the other major ferry operator in the Western Channel.

In a surprise press statement on 7th January 1994, it was announced that BCIF (who had formerly operated from Portsmouth) had been purchased by Commodore Shipping for an unknown figure following major losses during 1993.

Meanwhile, Commodore Ferries commissioned the building of a new £18 million freight ship for their Portsmouth-Guernsey-Jersey routes. The new 5,215-tonne freight ship would when commissioned replace the *Norman Commodore* on the link. The building of this new freight ship for the Channel Islands was the first new tonnage for over thirty years since British Rail ordered their vessels *Sarnia* and *Caesarea*.

As a result of the demise of British Channel Island Ferries, the *Purbeck* was brought under the management of Commodore Ferries to operate with the *Norman Commodore* and *Commodore Clipper*.

The Spanish service of P&O European

Ferries was to prove a great success, and her weekend calls to Cherbourg were to prove also successful in offering additional capacity on the link, especially during peak periods in the summer. The introduction of the *Pride of Bilbao* together with Brittany Ferries' winter service operated by the *Bretagne* from Portsmouth, were to see a major growth in the Spanish routes.

On 28th March 1994, P&O European Ferries secured a five-year charter of the Olau Line vessels *Olau Hollandia* and *Olau Britannia* from TT Line in Germany. Rumours of problems with the Olau service linking Sheerness and Vlissingen had been evident for some eighteen months. The ships had been carrying good loads but were not making sufficient profits for the parent company TT Line in Germany. It had been known for some time that P&O European Ferries wished to add both Olau ships to its fleet and place them on the Portsmouth-Le Havre service. Olau tried to make reductions in the manning costs of their vessels on the Kent/Dutch service, but without success, following strong German Seamen's Union resistance. The ships became too expensive for Olau Line to run, and in the event P&O European Ferries secured a five-year charter (with a further five-year option) for the twin ships. The *Olau Britannia* finished with the 21.30 sailing from Sheerness to Vlissingen on 12th May while the *Olau Hollandia* ended her operations on the route three days later.

The chartered ships emerged renamed as *Pride of Portsmouth* and *Pride of Le Havre* as long overdue tonnage required for P&O on their Le Havre operation. With a capacity for 575 cars, 423 cabins and berths for 1,642 passengers, both ships meant that the company was now able to compete against their major rivals Brittany Ferries with similar style and age of tonnage.

The *Pride of Portsmouth* entered service with P&O European Ferries on 31st May,

Commodore's freight vessel the ***Norman Commodore*** will be replaced during September 1995 by the first of the new purpose-built freight vessels being built for Commodore Shipping in Holland. *(Maritime Photographic)*

Ferries in all different sizes in the 90s. This view shows the ***Normandie***, ***Pride of Cherbourg*** and ***Pride of Portsmouth*** at the Continental Ferry Port in May 1994. *(Eric Brett)*

first undertaking a short charter for the MOD as part of the commemorations for the 50th Anniversary of the D-Day landings. Meanwhile, the *Pride of Le Havre* entered service four days later.

Problems with the construction of the new linkspan at Le Havre, and delays with the port facilities at the new terminal at the French port forced P&O European Ferries to put their newly acquired vessels into service initially on the Portsmouth-Cherbourg link with the *Pride of Cherbourg II* (formerly *Pride of Cherbourg*). P&O were unable to use the existing terminal with their new vessels at Le Havre as the linkspan was non-compatible. The light duty for the Cherbourg operation turned out possibly to be a blessing in disguise for the company, as it allowed both ships to settle down and give their crews time to acquaint themselves with the very different accommodation from that they had been used to working on for the last twenty years on the 'Super Viking' class ships.

On 22nd June, P&O European Ferries were able to transfer their new multi-million pound vessels to the Le Havre operation with completion of the £2.7 million terminal at the Normandy port.

The former Le Havre vessels, *Pride of Le Havre* (renamed *Pride of Cherbourg*) and *Pride of Hampshire* initially underwent short overhauls before replacing the smaller 'Super Vikings' on the Cherbourg route.

Following entry into service of the jumboised tonnage on the Cherbourg link, the *Pride of Winchester* was laid up for sale, while her counterpart the *Pride of Cherbourg II* was placed on freight runs with the *Gabriele Wehr* shadowing the new superferries on the Le Havre service.

Brittany Ferries were to see a four-fold increase in passenger traffic on their St.Malo route following the introduction of the *Bretagne*. The demand for the St.Malo service led the Company to open another route to the port from Poole using the *Duchesse Anne* as from May 1994.

Brittany Ferries' *Normandie* undertook two very interesting charters during the summer in 1994. In the June she was to transport the largest consignment of military vehicles to Normandy since the D-Day landings themselves as part of the 50th Anniversary celebrations. Later that summer as part of the 'Tour de France' she was chartered to transport the entourage on a special sailing between Portsmouth and Cherbourg.

The *Pride of Winchester*, with her sister *Pride of Cherbourg II*, were eventually sold by P&O European Ferries. The first to go, the 'Winchester', was sold to Greek interests and sailed from Portsmouth on 27th July 1994, renamed *V.Korneros*. Meanwhile, the *Pride of Cherbourg II* was later sold to Fred Olsen and renamed *Banderos*.

During the winter period of 1994, as in 1993, the *Val de Loire* was transferred from Roscoff to Caen to operate in tandem with the *Normandie*. Meanwhile, the *Bretagne* was employed again on the Spanish service from Portsmouth with just two round sailings to St.Malo during the winter period. Meanwhile, Brittany Ferries were considering building a second superferry vessel for the Caen route to partner the *Normandie*. The cost of such a vessel was

The ***Pride of Cherbourg II*** captured outward bound to Le Havre during her last season with P&O European Ferries. *(Miles Cowsill)*

An aerial view of the new Ferry Terminal at Le Havre with the ***Pride of Portsmouth*** at the linkspan. The ***Gabriele Wehr*** can be seen in the inner basin discharging freight.
(P&O European Ferries)

estimated to be around £82 million.

During the Christmas period, both the *Val de Loire* and the *Bretagne* undertook special cruises for Brittany Ferries, marketed as the 'City Cruises'. At Christmas, the *Bretagne* undertook a cruise to Rouen, and at New Year the *Val de Loire* was planned to sail to Amsterdam, but in the event sailed to Rouen instead due to bad weather in the North Sea.

Stena Sealink's Southampton-Cherbourg route, during the first eight months of 1994, achieved a 21% increase in passenger traffic and a 7% in freight units against the same period of 1993.

Meanwhile P&O European Ferries introduced additional freight tonnage on their Le Havre service in October, with the long-term charter of the *Thomas Wehr* to operate in tandem with the *Gabriele Wehr* on the link.

News broke during the autumn 1994 that P&O European Ferries were considering opening a Portsmouth-Bordeaux service in the near future. This news was shortly followed by the announcement that Brittany Ferries were undertaking a feasibility study to run a ferry service either from Portsmouth or Poole to Bayonne in the south of France.

It was also announced that Sea Containers were considering reintroducing their fast ferry service between Portsmouth and Cherbourg as from 1996, using one of the new super SeaCat craft on the link.

Portsmouth Continental Ferry Port has come a long way since the early days of spring 1976 when the *Viking Victory* and *Armorique* opened the initial operations to Cherbourg and St.Malo. Today the ferry port has the largest concentration of superferries in Britain, handling over thirty arrivals and departures during the peak season.

During late 1994, the Channel Tunnel opened its doors to traffic. Geographically Portsmouth should retain most of its present traffic on the routes to France and Spain. During the last twenty years, Portsmouth and its ferry operator partners have built up a fiercely loyal customer base among both leisure and commercial users. They have recognised the value of a regular, high quality service by the ferry operators to France and now Spain.

The prospect of further expansion combined with the challenge of the Channel Tunnel means that a fresh chapter will unfold in the continued and dynamic development of Portsmouth as a ferry port.

Above: The ***Val de Loire*** and ***Pride of Cherbourg*** captured in the winter sun at Portsmouth. *(Maritime Photographic)*

Below: Following the introduction of the new Superferries on the Portsmouth-Le Havre service, the former 'Super Vikings', the ***Pride of Cherbourg*** and ***Pride of Hampshire***, were transferred to the Portsmouth-Cherbourg service. *(Maritime Photographic)*

PORTSMOUTH THE PORT OF OPPORTUNITY

Richard Martin

A significant transformation has taken place in Portsmouth over the past few years that has led to the harbour becoming firmly established as a major British ferry port.

This transformation has seen the enlargement of the port together with improved facilities, but the greatest change, and certainly the most visual, is in the type of vessel now seen sailing through the harbour mouth at Portsmouth.

When P&O began its operations from Portsmouth, the ships weighed in at under 4,000 gross tonnes. Today, the largest cruiseferry ever to operate from Britain, P&O European Ferries' *Pride of Bilbao*, sails from Portsmouth with a gross tonnage of 37,583. Together with size has come an immense improvement in the type of facilities passengers can now enjoy, coupled with a standard and quality of service synonymous with P&O.

Significant changes together with massive investment began for P&O European Ferries in Portsmouth with the arrival in 1993 of the *Pride of Bilbao*. Her inaugural crossing to the northern Spanish port of Bilbao took place in April of that year. Since then we have seen a dramatic increase in the Spanish market and the number of passengers making use of our service has exceeded expectations. We have every reason to believe this is trend that will continue.

The company's investment continued with the arrival in June 1994 of the 33,336 tonnes sister ships *Pride of Portsmouth* and *Pride of Le Havre*. These ships, capable of carrying 1,600 passengers, have added significant capacity to our French routes - not only for passengers but also freight.

December 1994 saw us carry a record number of freight items on one day across our two French routes - this was made possible by the introduction of not only the two sister ships but also additional freight-only tonnage onto the Portsmouth-Le Havre service. We have also seen an increase in freight traffic on our Cherbourg route as a result of increased capacity. Freight plays a particularly important role in the overall economics of the company and we need to ensure that we meet all the requirements of the industry.

Investment is ongoing - not only in major ship refurbishment but also in staff training. P&O European Ferries became the biggest transport and travel company in the UK to be registered for BS 5750/ISO 9000 total quality management.

History has shown that the decision in

PORTSMOUTH-LE HAVRE

PARK LANE-ON-SEA.

P&O European Ferries two magnificent Cruiseferries from Portsmouth to Le Havre set new standards of luxury on the Western Channel.

In fact, they carry the Automobile Association 5 star rating.

Small wonder, considering all the facilities on board. There are 400 en-suite cabins, a choice of restaurants featuring an extensive buffet service or a self-service restaurant ideal for family dining. There are two bars and a night club, you can enjoy a dip in the pool, a film in the cinema or better still, a win in the casino. Which may come in handy as you browse through our on board shops, with their wide variety of luxurious fashion items, perfumes, gifts and duty-free goods.

Furthermore, we provide an area ideal for families with the self-service restaurant nearby, refreshments served 24 hours a day and a play area and video games for the children

In short, our Cruiseferries have all the luxuries you usually find in a 5 star hotel. And, of course, some you don't.

Such as sun decks with fresh sea air and superb sea views.

For reservations, brochures or further information please call (01705) 827677.

BRITAIN'S No. 1 FERRY COMPANY

Pride of Le Havre *(Ferry Publications Library)*

1976 to move the company's operation from Southampton to Portsmouth has certainly proved to have been the correct one. Portsmouth is an hour's shorter sailing time to France, enabling us to offer three round trips a day instead of two. The motorway brings the driver to our doorstep and with improvements throughout the UK road network, Portsmouth is easily accessible via motorway or dual carriageway from virtually all parts of the country. The City Council has also invested in enlarging the port to accommodate greater quantities of freight - essential if the port is to continue to be successful.

All this does not necessarily mean that Portsmouth is 100% perfect! However, we are working together with the City Council and port officials on those areas that need improvement.

There is no doubt that the Channel Tunnel will significantly change the face of the ferry industry (once it is fully operational). I believe the greatest changes will take place on the short sea sector, but only time will tell what real effect the tunnel will have on shipping companies.

The tremors will be felt here in Portsmouth but we have finely honed our operation to meet this latest challenge. The tunnel will not be able to offer the service and quality that we can provide on our AA five star ships. The shuttle will be a very basic service and for those passengers who want to relax, take a meal, sleep or just let the children stretch their legs, then the ferries will still be the answer.

Portsmouth also benefits from geography. A family from the Midlands would surely rather use the ever-improving road links to Portsmouth than spend hours struggling to Folkestone. The Channel Tunnel will certainly have a 'novelty value', but once this has worn off people will return to the ferries.

P&O European Ferries has made a large investment in its operations from Portsmouth and I am confident in the future of the port's ferry industry

Richard Martin, Managing Director of P&O European Ferries (Portsmouth) Ltd..

Pride of Portsmouth and **_Pride of Le Havre_**
(FotoFlite)

PENCIL & PIECE OF STRING LEADS TO PORTSMOUTH FERRY SUCCESS

The story of Portsmouth ferry port is an interesting one in which Brittany Ferries has been, and no doubt will continue to be, intimately involved. It all began with a piece of string and a pencil, so the story goes.

In 1975 the Bretons announced a plan to re-open the historic link with the UK from St.Malo. The original line to Southampton had been closed some years before, having gained some notoriety as the escape route used by Soviet spies Burgess and MacLean. The French company had to find a port in the UK that would allow them to make a return crossing in 24 hours with sufficient time in port to load and discharge using a ship of around 18 knots. Taking these facts into account, and using the piece of string and pencil, an arc was drawn from St.Malo and found to cut through both Weymouth and Portsmouth!

Portsmouth was the preferred choice but, at that time, there was no ferry port. Working in association with Commodore Shipping, Brittany Ferries made an approach to Portsmouth City Council in the early part of 1975 to see if they would be interested in developing facilities for a service to St.Malo. At that time Brittany Ferries owned only one small ship, the *Penn-Ar-Bed*, operating between Plymouth and Roscoff, and the City Fathers looked around to see if they could provide more substance to the development and approached the then Townsend Thoresen

Ian.A. Carruthers

in Southampton. Anticipating the effects of a new service to St.Malo, Townsend Thoresen agreed to a seasonal operation from Portsmouth, diverting a service from Southampton really as a safeguard to their Cherbourg route, rather than an extension of their overall operations.

Due to government planning restrictions, the port at Portsmouth had to be built for less than £1m and, by the time all the agreements were in place, there were only 100 days in which to construct it.

I joined Brittany Ferries at about that time to experience the usual difficulties in any project of this nature, and was there to see the port open 100 days later in June 1976. The later part of that year was an interesting period during which Brittany Ferries was the only operator in the port and faced great opposition from Southampton dock workers, who believed that their own employment would be

CAFE SOCIETY

DIRECT TO HOLIDAY FRANCE AND SPAIN.

With Brittany Ferries, your holiday starts the moment you step aboard our award-winning, luxury cruise-ferries.

From our easily reached ports in the UK, we'll speed you direct to Holiday France and Spain.

You'll discover we're so much closer to all the most delightful holiday areas of France – Brittany, Normandy, the Loire Valley, Dordogne, Aquitaine and further south, Provence and the Mediterranean.

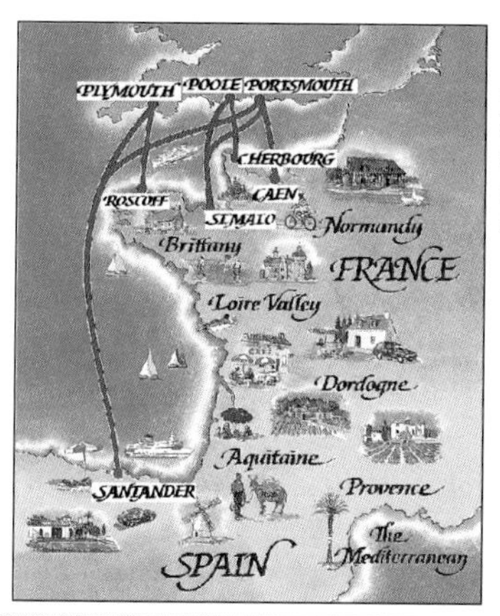

Our exciting brochures are packed with ideas and facts about our wide range of sailings and fares, holidays and breaks all offering excellent value, including some very special offers.

Information & Reservations
(01705) 827701
24 hour brochure service
(01752) 269926
or see your travel agent.

Armorique *(FotoFlite)*

threatened if the company's ferry *Armorique*, capable of carrying 16 lorries, was allowed to operate a daily winter service from Portsmouth. They were right, but for the wrong reasons!

However, after weeks of nightly scenes reminiscent of the miners' dispute, a settlement was eventually reached and Brittany Ferries pressed ahead with its pioneering service. Following a period of fairly rapid growth in 1981, Brittany Ferries contracted for what was to be termed 'Phase 3', consisting of substantial reclamation work, and which in fact became the catalyst for all the major work subsequently undertaken to date. The expansion was required in order to provide the necessary infrastructure for a new route to Caen. The additional land area and berth was duly delivered in the course of 1984, although it was a further two years before the route to Caen was established.

It is now a matter of history, but the route that was the subject of a lot of opposition and thought by the other operators to be unnecessary, became the largest ferry route on the Channel outside the Dover Straits. It also proved, yet again, the Brittany Ferries' belief that there was substantial potential for services on the Western Channel, if totally new routes were developed to take people where they wanted to go rather than historically where it had been commercially preferable to 'drop them off'.

Having established the new service in 1986 the next major phase of development was the decision to construct a berth for the future generation of Jumbo cruise ferries. Again, Brittany Ferries was at the forefront of this decision and undertook yet again to support and guarantee the construction of these large berths, culminating in late Spring 1992 in the introduction into service of the first of the new generation ferries on the Western Channel in the form of the *Normandie*. (The port now has a greater concentration of large cruise ferries than any other port in Northern Europe.)

Brittany Ferries are very proud of the part they have played in the development of Portsmouth and the fact that on each occasion they were responsible for taking the first step. Whilst growth at the port has tended to outstrip available space, the recent acquisition of more land enables us to look forward to being able to provide fast and efficient routing through the port for our passengers and freight clients alike, compatible with the standards and expectations of the 90's and into the next millennium.

Brittany Ferries remains totally committed to Portsmouth, and plans are advanced to invest in more re-fleeting programmes so that vessels operating from the port will be of a uniform cruise ferry standard.

As well as a principal port in our network Portsmouth is also the home of a substantial part of our commercial structure, with a large reservations centre handling up to 5,000 calls per day. Our commitment and investment will continue as well as the innovation and dynamism that began with a piece of string and a pencil some twenty years ago. Or so the story goes.

Ian. A. Carruthers,
Managing Director (UK & Ireland)

Normandie *(Miles Cowsill)*

STENA SEALINK LINE

The Southampton-Cherbourg route is of major strategic importance to Stena Sealink Line as we continue our philosophy of maintaining a wide network of services rather than becoming over-dependent on a single route or sector.

Whilst our return to the Western Channel is still relatively recent, with just three peak seasons behind us, we are now benefiting from growing awareness of the route, and customers are heading for the service from an increasingly wide catchment area.

The service received maximum attention in 1994 with a more aggressive marketing campaign and a substantial increase in capacity by expanding the period of twice-daily services from Whitsun right through to the third week of September.

The results speak for themselves: in 1994 passenger carryings jumped 20% - the biggest percentage increase on any route within the entire Stena Line group - to almost 600,000.

Freight carryings rose a healthy 6% to almost 15,000 units, and we must actively consider additional tonnage, initially for the peak tourist season, if we are to maintain this performance.

The *Stena Normandy* is perfect for the service. She is one of the largest cruise ferries operating in British waters, combining massive cabin accommodation with a range of public facilities along the lines of a top international hotel. The ship was extensively re-fitted before transferring to the route and was substantially upgraded during her 1995 winter re-fit at A&P Appledore, benefiting from improvements to the shopping areas, new galleys and widespread general refurbishment of fixtures and fittings.

Ashore, the Southampton terminal was extensively upgraded in 1994 and a new terminal has opened at Cherbourg.

W. G. Cooper

The style of service on the Western Channel contrasts dramatically with the pace of ferry services on the short-sea crossings to France. Motorists starting their holiday with an overnight sailing to Normandy from Southampton have ample time to rest and relax, dine in fine style and be royally entertained in the nightclub, bar and restaurant facilities the *Stena Normandy* has to offer.

But, looking to the future, we must consider the route as a candidate for a more streamlined service using one of our new Stena HSS high speed superferries.

The length of crossing makes the Southampton-Cherbourg service an appealing candidate for one of these craft. The prospect of reducing the present five hour crossing by half with one of these 40 knot vessels is substantial, raising exciting new possibilities for short breaks and day trip business.

Gareth Cooper

W G Cooper, Managing Director,
Stena Sealink Line

They all point to the world's leading ferry company.

Stena Sealink Line, part of Stena Line, the world's leading and largest ferry company, offers you a route to the whole of Europe.

By traditional ferry, fast catamaran or the new revolutionary Stena High-speed Sea Service, Stena Sealink will point you in the right direction.

To book call now on 01233 647047 or contact your local travel agent or motoring organisation.

STENA LINE - THE WORLD'S LEADING FERRY COMPANY

THE VITAL EVERYDAY LINK

Today Commodore Ferries operates three conventional freight vessels to Jersey and Guernsey. It was not until 1989 that we made the move to ro-ro vessels, prior to that we had operated a conventional container service to the Islands on a daily basis from Portsmouth.

The three sailings per day to Jersey and Guernsey depart from number one linkspan situated at the ferryport terminal, Portsmouth, with the trailer holding area being located at the Albert Johnson Quay. The *Norman Commodore*, which can accommodate 45 x 12m trailers, sails to Jersey from Portsmouth every morning at 09.30 via Guernsey, returning to Portsmouth at night.The *Purbeck*, which has a capacity of 57 x 12m trailers, leaves Portsmouth at night, reaching St. Helier at 06.00, and the *Commodore Clipper*, which has the same capacity as the *Norman Commodore*, provides a nightly service to St. Peter Port. It is essential that we operate two overnight vessels to the islands, which ensures that clients receive an early arrival of goods in both Guernsey and Jersey.

The company also operates a weekly service between Guernsey-Jersey-St.Malo every Friday, which is a vital link for both the islanders and the Breton community.

Currently Commodore Ferries has two new vessels on order in Holland. The first of these, to be named *Island Commodore*, is due to enter service during May 1995 and will be able to carry 95 x 12m trailers with have a capacity for 12 driver passengers. The second of the vessels, yet to be named, is due to enter service during March 1996.

No final decision has been made about the retention of the current vessels in the fleet, but we expect to maintain the *Purbeck* until January 1998, the *Norman Commodore* until at least September 1995.

Jeff Vidamour

Currently Commodore Ferries handles 50,000 freight units and 25,000 cars a year on their Channel Islands services.. Whilst there is a steady all-year round trade from the mainland to Jersey and Guernsey, possibly the busiest time for us as a shipping company with trade to the UK is during the spring, when we handle the early spring crops of tomatoes, potatoes and spring flowers.

Portsmouth is an ideal port for Commodore Ferries geographically, as it offers ideal road communications to the rest of the country. We are committed to Portsmouth as our ferry link to the Channel Islands. Our long-term commitment for hauliers and the islanders alike has been clearly illustrated in the investment in the two new vessels we have ordered in Holland.

J. Vidamour

Jeff Vidamour
Managing Director, Commodore Ferries

A TWICE DAILY ROLL ON ROLL OFF SHIPPING SERVICE

LONDON
SOUTHAMPTON
PORTSMOUTH
WEYMOUTH
CHERBOURG
GUERNSEY
JERSEY
ST. MALO
RENNES

FROM PORTSMOUTH TO BOTH GUERNSEY AND JERSEY

FOR FULL DETAILS CONTACT

COMMODORE FERRIES LIMITED
COMMODORE HOUSE
ST. SAMPSONS, GUERNSEY GY1 3AF
TEL (0481) 46841
FAX (0481) 49543

A SUPERFERRY IS BORN

In May 1990 Brittany Ferries announced plans to build two new superferries to replace some of the older tonnage in the fleet and to expand both the Portsmouth-Caen and Poole-Cherbourg services. The contract for the first vessel, a cruise ferry for the Caen operation, was awarded to Masa yards in Finland. The second contract for a new ship for Brittany Ferries' subsidiary Truckline passenger operation out of Poole was also awarded to Masa. Together the orders were worth some £130 million and each new ship was to take some two years to build.

Shortly after the Caen ship was announced, I was appointed as her Senior Master and Landsman in the Project Department at our head office in Roscoff.

Bertrand Apperry

It was Spring 1991 when I first travelled to Turku in Finland to witness the laying of the first of the keel blocks. It was a splendid crystal clear Scandinavian morning when the yard's Project Manager Mr Ilka Seppa and I laid a plastic bag containing newly minted Finnish and French coins on the first keel block. The bag was carefully fastened on the top of the block to support the total weight of the construction of the

The ***Normandie*** under construction in Finland. *(Bertrand Apperry)*

ship prior to her launch.

After the launch of the *Normandie*, as she was to be named, the coins were removed for a further ceremony organised by the shipyard. The original bag of coins was then placed at the next ceremony in a steel box aft of the main mast on the bridge. Included in the box was a list of signatures of all the people present.

Over the next year I was to witness the building of the massive superferry with my Chief Engineer, Michel Lasvaladas. Following the floating of the vessel in the dock, she was removed to a fitting-out basin for the final stages of her construction. During March 1992, not the best time of the year for weather in Finland, we headed for the open seas for first trials. Before our departure, a further ceremony took place on board during which a small icon was placed on the main engine room controls desk close to the power control and another placed on the bridge above the main chart table.

The Finnish builders delivered the elegant *Normandie* on time. Prior to us making our maiden voyage between Caen and Portsmouth, we carried out several public relations exercises. We enjoyed a leisurely cruise from Finland through the Baltic into the North Sea to the Netherlands where we made our first stop. Originally the naming of the *Normandie* was going to take place at Caen but unfortunately, what I will call here exceptional circumstances prevented this, and the official ceremony took place at Rotterdam. The Christening of the *Normandie* was led by a Breton priest in the presence of the 'Godmother' of the vessel, Madame Garrec of Caen. After this short ceremony, we set sail again towards the vessel's home port of Ouistreham, Caen's coastal ferry port, for berthing trials. Next day we headed for Portsmouth. As I manoeuvred the giant new vessel into

Normandie - Information Area *(Brittany Ferries)*

'Pompey', the whole of the population of the famous south coast port appeared to have turned out for the event, no doubt interested to see whether I was going to put the first scratch on the ship's gleaming white paintwork! Earlier as we had slipped through the port entrance, the graceful little *Armorique* on which I had been captain for many years went past us on one of her last official sailings under the Brittany Ferries flag. I thought then how things had changed over the years I had been with the company.

That evening my officers and I entertained a VIP party of journalists and travel trade executives on a cruise down the Solent. The June evening was magnificent and all too soon the gala was over and *Normandie* had to start earning her keep. The next day we carried out the ship's first commercial sailing.

The *Normandie* has established herself well on the Caen service and is much the envy of other ferry operators. After two years she remains the youngest and undoubtedly the best looking ferry on the English Channel with safety, comfort, cleanliness, quality of onboard experience, speed of loading and punctuality again the envy of other operators!

We have a faithful band of passengers who regularly like to travel on the *Normandie*, some have even travelled more than seventy times on the ship. On board we try to offer something a little different for our customers, including regular bridge visits and trips to the engine room and galley which I have inaugurated this year. Table tennis competitions, a shuffle-board game on the sun-deck – just like on prestigious cruise liners – seaman's knot practice and plenty of children's entertainment can all be enjoyed on our six hour crossings.

In addition during the winter months, we have Sky TV with special lounges set aside for passengers to watch international sporting events on Sky Sports. Once a week, the Chief Engineer and I have dinner in the restaurant in the company of some of the passengers travelling on board the ship. I have introduced this dinner on the Captain's table as it gives me an opportunity to hear first hand, the views of my passengers.

Now some figures regarding the graceful *Normandie*. After only two and a half years, this successful ship has carried 1.5 million passengers, sailed more than 227,000 nautical miles (10.5 times around the world!) in 2,270 trips across the English Channel.

At the end of this year, I will take my leave of *Normandie* and Brittany Ferries after seventeen years. I have commanded ten ships and have a pilotage licence for seven ports. I have sailed the Channel in all weathers and come September when it is time to go I will do so with great sadness.

I sincerely hope that I will have the pleasure of seeing you before my departure from *Normandie*. You are more than welcome aboard my ship any time.

Bertrand Apperry
Senior Captain,
Normandie

THE THREE CLASSES OF SHIP CONCEPT

Tony Shopland

In the beginning ......

As each year passes, so another decade advances, and the fascinating history of roll-on/roll-off ferries recedes but must never be forgotten. In previous publications we have explored the foundation, successes, amalgamations and conversions of our fleets on the Western routes.

Today I have been asked to describe the concept of the 'three classes or generations' of ship during my 'lifetime' of service across the English Channel.

In the beginning, or as far back as one would wish to remember, for myself that is over a quarter of a century, we saw the first roll-on/roll-off or 'drive through' ferries in service across the Channel. In those days we believed the vessels to be extremely large, fast and an efficient mode of transport across the waters between England and France, which, compared to previous methods, of 'craning' vehicles on

Viking I *(Ray Sprake Collection)*

Above: **Pride of Portsmouth** *(Miles Cowsill)*
Below: Buffet Restaurant - **Pride of Le Havre** *(Miles Cowsill)*

and off, was indeed a major innovation in the maritime transport industry.

At a mere 99 metres in length from bow to stern, a beam of 18 metres and a loaded draught of 4.5 metres, these ferries could carry nearly one thousand passengers and the equivalent of 180 single cars at a speed of 19 knots, in relative comfort. In those pioneering days, to the average family every voyage was an adventure, exploring another country - France and beyond. The one important factor then was that the average family car measured just over 3 metres, whereas today we talk in terms of an average length of over 5 metres. At the outset this point would not appear too important, unless of course you have a small garage! To us it is a very critical factor in the planning and operation of our 'floating car parks'!

As a transport facility, we also have to provide for the all important needs of a real commercial world, the movement of materials and goods in an ever-increasing international market. Thus in the original designs of our ships, equivalent attention was paid to the carriage of self-driven cargo vehicles and unaccompanied freight units. In this area alone we include shipments of standard trailers, new or export cars, agricultural machinery, caravans, and today even mobile homes, as large as they are. in fact, we have to consider shipping anything on wheels!

So, by the end of the sixties, the scene was set, routes established, the Norwegian flagged '*Vikings I, II, III* and *IV*' were well proved and our clients were "appetised" to the continental scene. Had we believed this first generation of ferries - the original 'Viking class' - was the ultimate in short sea transport, I would not be here at my desk writing this article today.

The world was rapidly advancing, and the dawning of the seventies saw increasing competition on Channel routes, with the introduction of a mixture of short sea shipping companies, vessels and ideas. None of these, as it now transpires, posed any long term threat to the already well established Anglo/Norwegian enterprise.

Within our own organisation, we did not stand still. The chances of investment in new tonnage were good, and our financial advisers were happy, or at least as satisfied as one ever sees an accountant!

Thus by the mid seventies, we were operating our 'second generation' ferries, I then recall, in a fleet of some twenty four ships within the corporate body of the company, the average age of each vessel was just four years, which was considered to be a very 'young flotilla'.

What was the 'Second Generation'? Well, obviously it was broadly based on the first series, but with many modifications, modelled on the experiences learned in the previous decade, but still with a very strong Scandinavian input, being also built in Denmark.

The main or outstanding features, of course, were increase in size, versatility, comfort and the ever-increasing need to improve facilities for our customers.

The 'Super Viking' Class, four of a series, boasted an increase in capacity of some 53% over their older Norwegian sisters, measured in terms of the number of vehicles each could carry. For an increase in hull length of just 30 metres and 2 metres more beam, the extra carrying ability was achieved by full width car platforms within the main vehicle deck area, plus an additional 'garage' deck which could accommodate fifty or so single cars above and apart from the main deck space.

The cranes position for the first stage of the jumboisation of the ***Viking Venturer***.
(Ferry Publications Library)

Although just ten years younger than their predecessors, advanced technology, operating systems and furnishings went into the new buildings in order to maintain and even improve upon the very high standards to which we were already operating.

Also built into these four sister ships was a certain level of versatility or flexibility never yet seen in modern ship technology, for it was during the era of off season (winter) charter hires, when our ships could be transferred to just about any ferry port in northern Europe, either to relieve our own fleet for annual refits/refurbishments or more lucratively to be 'hired' by another company, or even HM Government for various interesting exercises in support of our military organisations. In those days we even visited outports just to publicise our own product. Previously, in order to achieve the degree of flexibility, whenever we had to operate from an 'alien' berth, our loading ramps had to have major 'surgery' in order to fit, which entailed cutting, rewelding and shaping areas of steelwork so that vehicles could embark and disembark safely and efficiently. These modifications of course took time both prior to and following the charter, and were similarly costly. Hence with the 'Super Vikings' we built, the bow and stern ramps could, in a couple of hours work by ship's staff, be modified by a series of hydraulic interlocks, integral bolt on-bolt off sections, pins etc, be transformed to fit in the majority of cases. This transformation would take place in less time than the sea passage between the operating and charter ports.

Although this article is about the three generations or classes of ship, in fact I can now cheat a little and cover an extra half generation.

By the end of the 1970's, the Super Vikings had proved to be an ideal carrier, both in term of passengers and freight. With a three main engine/propeller configuration and good ship handling characteristics, coupled with, as always within our fleets, a first class maintenance policy, the ships held up well to a very full daily schedule, seven days a week and on average fifty weeks per year, stopping only for a two-week annual refit. But, as was the case just ten years previously, demand was rapidly outstripping supply, and although we were supplementing our routes with chartered-in freighters, a more long term solution had to be found. This time though, the financial scene was different, the accountants really were not smiling!

To design and build new tonnage in the early 1980's was financially prohibitive so we decided to convert or 'jumboise' two ships for the Portsmouth-Le Havre route - *Viking Venturer* and *Viking Valiant*. Similarly our colleagues at Dover carried out the same project on two of their sister ships *Free Enterprises VI* and *VII*. Using the same shipyard at Bremerhaven in Germany, we witnessed an incredible transformation of two pairs of vessels within a very short period, and thus by the mid-season of 1986, just four months off service, we had the equivalent of two new ferries, completely refurbished and with an effective carrying capacity doubled, especially on freight space. Hence the two jumbos were scheduled for our very busy Portsmouth-Le Havre route.

The complete project, from drawing board to re-delivery, carried out on our two sister ships took less than one year to achieve. The operation was staggered, that is one ship 'led' the other by about four weeks, each vessel being out of service no longer than twenty weeks, during a quiet operating period; and the total cost was a mere fraction of the cost of one new build.

Mechanically, the jumbos, as they were so called, were the same as before, three main engines turning three CPP propellers. The length overall was increased from 129 metres to 144 metres by fitting a new bow section, but the main 'expansion' was in the fitting of a complete through vehicle deck between the existing main deck and the superstructure or passenger decks. The overall life of the ships was then extended by between five and ten years over and above their original life expectancy, and at least well into the next century. Although some have said the final profile was not very

Pride of Bilbao *(Miles Cowsill)*

pleasing to the eye, the end result was extremely functional, enabling us to load and discharge the two vehicle decks simultaneously with no requirement to lengthen our time in port. Mariners very quickly learn that any ship does not earn its keep when it is tied up in port.

So the eighties ended, and we witnessed many changes in shipping companies, new routes being explored, new styles of managing and marketing techniques, in fact anything to persuade our clients that this is still the best way to travel. Competition was still very high and with the advancing threat of the 'tunnel', we very quickly realised that even the jumbos would not be sufficient to meet market demands.

The beginning of 1990 saw management teams once again gazing into their crystal balls, but the accountants were still not really satisfied. In order to survive the ever advancing market we had to look to the future, which wasn't easy. Should we rationalise or prepare to meet the tunnel 'head on'. For us seafarers the future looked bleak. Investment in new tonnage was, as in the eighties, prohibitive. The only hope was to search the existing markets. One had to be very patient, especially as shipmasters we were not party to the private and complex negotiations of shipowners. However we had to motivate staff and customers alike, that, given time, improvements would be forthcoming.

Just two years into this decade something was 'afoot', management was probing, questions were being asked, "if we should do this ... could this be achieved?". Harbour authorities were in consultation, port engineers were taking measurements, what could be the largest ferry that could safely and efficiently operate from this port? Those above us had to be convinced that it would work given the huge outlay required.

Well, by the spring of 1993, we were all to witness the beginning of the latest era in modern ferrying and mini-cruising. Long and sleepless nights were had by all. Finally the largest ferry to operate in British waters arrived at Portsmouth from Swedish waters, to take up a new service to Spain, the renamed *Pride of Bilbao*, described as a Baltic cruise ferry. This was the beginning of a new concept on our channel routes.

As if this was not enough to contend with-a brand new service to the Iberian Peninsula - we still had to look to our home routes for modernisation. With the experiences of the *Pride of Bilbao* inauguration very fresh in our minds, there was yet another light on the horizon, two in fact.

A pair of sister ships, just four years old, built on similar lines to the 'Baltic' class, became available for charter in 1994. Unlike any form of roll-on/roll-off vessel we have seen on our Western routes, similar in dimensions to the *Pride of Bilbao*, these two sisters - *Olau Britannia* and *Olau Hollandia*, were the ultimate in cruise ferry travel, having already earned five star classification whilst on service in the southern North Sea.

With only minor modifications to be made, including of course the changing of company logo, and a hull repaint, the major task was training ships staff in new techniques and up to date management systems.

Within a period of eight weeks or so, with the two ships laid up in the port of Le Havre, we had trained over three hundred officers and crew in modern ship operations, changed the flag state to the

Red Ensign and trialled the berths and linkspans from which we were due to operate. Port facilities, being an all important and costly factor in any ship operation, also required much forward planning and capital outlay by the relevant port authority in order to accommodate company vessels.

Thus we have arrived at the so called 'Third Generation', as we see it on the Western Channel routes.

Similar to a floating hotel, the most noticeable innovation is in the overall ship management. Previous series of ferries were relatively small and easy to manage with small teams of crew. Even captains were seen to lend a hand at busy times in passenger spaces, when 'pressure points' required easing.

Today the scene is different, ships masters head an on-board management team of four senior officers who in turn have to run their respective departments, having within each group up to ten managers, as for example in the hotel services department.

In summarising, and in conclusion, the two themes which run throughout, the secret of a good service to our travelling public, the keyword for the success of a reputable company to which I am fortunate to have been a part of for the past twenty years, are TEAMWORK and RESPECT.

As a TEAM we work together to provide the best possible service to our customers, and in doing so we are able to RESPECT the needs of our clients in their transportation across these busy channel waters.

Captain Tony Shopland
Pride of Portsmouth

The ***Pride of Le Havre*** and ***Pride of Portsmouth*** pass each other in mid-channel. *(FotoFlite)*

ISLE OF WIGHT SERVICES

The history of Red Funnel, one of the current operators to the Isle of Wight, can be traced back to 1820. The first steamer on the link between Southampton and Cowes was placed on the route in the same year using the vessel *Prince of Coburg*. Some six years later, the Southampton authorities decided to start their own service to rival the island based operation, as they considered the company was monopolising the route. A year later, both companies decided to work together in an effort to save money and by 1861, both rival operations had joined forces to form a company called Southampton, Isle of Wight & Portsmouth Improved Steam Boat Company. By 1885, they had acquired its first tug, when they purchased the new Southampton Steam Navigation Company. This side of the company still continues today, handling the many movements of the port of Southampton.

In 1908, the company acquired the Bournemouth & South Coast Steam Packets Limited, further strengthening its position on the Solent and the south coast with the excursion market. They continued to expand their operations until the Second World War with new vessels and excursion routes. Following the end of hostilities in 1945, the company was forced to purchase a number of second-hand vessels to maintain their operations, including a former tank landing craft used during the war which was to carry the *Norris Castle*. It became evident in the early fifties that the excursion market was becoming less viable, and by 1952 the fleet had been pruned, with motor vessels being used primarily and excursion work becoming very much a secondary consideration within the group.

With the rapid development in the fifties and the sixties of Fawley Oil Terminal in the Southampton Water, and the docks at Southampton at their height of trade with cargo and liner traffic, additional tugs were purchased to maintain operations. By November 1957 the chief revenue for the company was being earned from the tug operation in the Solent, secondly from the Southampton-East and West Cowes service, and thirdly from the excursion work which was still in decline.

The emerging holiday with the family car saw Red Funnel order their first post-war passenger car ferry in 1957. The vessel, named *Carisbrooke Castle*, entered service some two years later, boasting a capacity of 45 cars. Her entry into service followed in the sixties with the introduction of further new tonnage which is covered in further detail later in this chapter.

In 1989, Associated British Ports (ABP), owners of the Port of Southampton, acquired Red Funnel Ferries. As a result of this takeover new vessels were built for the company to replace the ageing sixties fleet.

The other operations to the Isle of Wight, Portsmouth-Ryde and Lymington-Yarmouth are also steeped in an interesting web of history. The car ferry service between Portsmouth and Fishbourne historically is the youngest of the links to the Isle of Wight, but is possibly one of the busiest of them in the nineties as one of the major gateways for both commerce and the holiday traffic.

The Lymington-Yarmouth route was originally set up by the independent Lymington Railway Company in 1858. Some nineteen years later the London & South Western Railway Company took control of the operation. Five years later the pier at

Red Funnel's car ferry ***Norris Castle*** leaves Cowes on the afternoon sailing to Southampton. *(FotoFlite)*

Lymington was extended, allowing crossings to Yarmouth to be undertaken at all stages of the tide. A series of vessels maintained the link until 1923, when the Southern Railway Company was formed and took control of the service. In 1927, the largest and the last paddle steamer to be constructed for the company was built on the Isle of Wight for the link. The *Freshwater* was to remain with the company until 1959, when she was sold for further operations on the south coast.

With the changing market, especially with more holiday-makers wanting to take their cars to the Island, the first car ferry was built for the route in 1938. The new double-ended ferry, named the *Lymington*, entered service in May 1938, boasting a capacity for 400 passengers and 16 cars. She was to be the first British ferry to be built with the now standard Voith Schneider propulsion. Following the end of the Second World War, the diesel electric paddle vessel *Farringford* was introduced with a capacity for 32 cars and 320 passengers.

Car and passenger traffic continued to expand on the Lymington-Yarmouth service during the fifties and as a result a third car ferry, the *Freshwater*, was introduced. Further expansion in the sixties, including improvements to enlarge the shore facilities, were undertaken to improve the expanding passenger and car traffic to the Isle of Wight.

Meanwhile, the Portsmouth-Ryde service can be traced back to the 18th century when a once-a-day sailing boat service commenced between both ports. The Portsmouth-Ryde Steam Packet Company had established their own service by the 1820s. In order to accommodate larger vessels, Ryde Pier was extended in 1824. The Pier was also to be the base for destinations other than Portsmouth. By 1830, the Southampton-Cowes-Ryde-Portsmouth service had been established. In addition to these regular services, Ryde was to be the centre of many calls of excursion vessels operating in the Solent and along the south coast.

Sealink's car ferry ***Freshwater*** seen here arriving at Portsmouth Harbour in March 1982. *(David Marshall)*

At Portsmouth, operations were focused originally on the Victoria Pier at Old Portsmouth which opened to traffic in May 1842 and steadily grew in popularity until the Clarence Pier at Southsea was opened. Meanwhile, the Albert Pier was built in 1846, allowing vessels to land and embark at all states of the tide. Portsmouth Harbour station now occupies this site.

In the autumn of 1872, a rival operation was started on the Solent offering a half-hourly service between Southsea and Ryde. Eventually, as on the Southampton-Cowes service, both competitors were to merge their operations. In 1879, the London & South Western and Brighton & South Western Railways applied to Parliament for a Bill allowing them to operate a ferry service between Portsmouth and the Isle of Wight. Some three years earlier, the line between Portsmouth town and the harbour station had been opened.

The established operator, the United Company, decided to order a new vessel to take on the new rival service operated by the railways. In the event, the railway companies were to succeed, having an advantage over them with a direct ferry service from Portsmouth Harbour station to Ryde, where passengers were able to transfer again from ship to train to other railway destinations on the Isle of Wight. In the light of further fierce competition, both rival railway companies decided to order new tonnage for their Portsmouth-Ryde service, which would be faster than the rivals. The railway companies also planned to purchase the whole of the Isle of Wight railway system in addition to the new railway pier at Ryde, then under construction. In the light of this, both running powers on the Ryde-Portsmouth link, plus the United Company fleet of seven vessels were sold to the railway companies. Following the takeover, a regular pattern of services was established between Portsmouth and Ryde. New and larger vessels were introduced for the ever-increasing market of passengers to the island.

Prior to the outbreak of the Second World War, seven paddle steamers were employed on the Portsmouth/Southsea services to Ryde. The vessels were also utilised on excursions along the south coast and in the Solent.

A wonderful nostalgic view of the ***Southsea*** and ***Brading*** passing each other at the entrance to Portsmouth Harbour in June 1979. *(David Marshall)*

Following the end of hostilities, Southern Railway ordered two new passenger ships to maintain the Ryde service. The twin screw motor vessels *Southsea* and *Brading* were built by Denny of Dumbarton and entered service in 1948. Both ships, and later a third sister, the *Shanklin*, were to become very much part of the Solent scene until the early eighties. British Railways, who took over operations from Southern Railway in 1948, were to discover also like Red Funnel that the heyday of excursions in the Solent and the south coast was on the decline in the early fifties; this eventually saw operations reduced in line with demand.

1958-1969

In November 1958, the *Carisbrooke Castle* entered the water at Southampton for Red Funnel. She was built at a cost of some £300,000, with an operating speed of some 14.7 knots, allowing her to operate between Southampton and Cowes in 45 minutes. She was to be the mainstay of the car-ferry service with the ex-LCT vessel the *Norris Castle*, with a capacity for 45 cars. During her first six months in service, she was to carry some 195,515 passengers, 15,829 cars and some 3,147 commercial vehicles. The ship was voted a great success and was to be joined some four years later by her new running partner, the *Osborne Castle*. Both vessels were then to lead a fairly uneventful time maintaining the operations together on the run between Southampton and Cowes.

Meanwhile, Red Funnel's rivals, British Railways, had introduced the *Farringford* in 1948, to operate with the smaller double-ended vessel *Lymington*, on the Yarmouth-Lymington route. With increased traffic on this link, a third ferry, the *Freshwater,* was introduced in 1959, which could accommodate some 26 cars and 620 passengers. Meanwhile on the other car ferry route to the island between Portsmouth and Fishbourne, British Rail introduced two new ferries in 1961 to replace smaller and older tonnage from the thirties. The two new vessels, the *Fishbourne* and *Camber Queen*, were able to accommodate some 34 cars and 168 passengers on the forty minute crossing.

Meanwhile passenger-only operations between Portsmouth and Ryde of British Rail was maintained in the sixties by the splendid looking *Brading*, *Southsea* and *Shanklin*, and also the smaller and distinctive looking paddle steamer *Ryde*. The level of traffic between the mainland and the island in the sixties required four vessels, especially on Saturdays. British Rail, like their competitors Red Funnel, were to offer limited cruises in the Solent and along the south coast, but it was becoming more and more evident that the cruise market was in decline. In September 1969, the paddle steamer *Ryde* was withdrawn from service, partly due to her age, but also with the decline in passenger traffic it was considered that the three passenger ships would be able to cope with operations in the future.

The passenger-only service of Red Funnel was maintained as from 1949 by the *Balmoral*, which was designed specifically for the route with limited car capacity, with excursion and tender work also in mind. The *Balmoral* proved a valiant workhorse for the company and in 1963, the company were considering converting her to a car ferry in order for them to meet the ever-growing demand of motorists wanting to take their cars to the Isle of Wight. In the event it was decided that the ship was unsuitable for conversion.

In December 1965, the third new car ferry was introduced by Red Funnel. Virtually similar to the *Osborne Castle*, the *Cowes Castle* was a welcomed addition to the fleet. Three years later, a fourth 'Castle' Class vessel was ordered, and was to be of a similar design to the three previous ships, but with the reduced passenger capacity in order for her to be able to carry more freight vehicles. She was named *Norris Castle* by Mrs R W B Lacon, owner of Norris Castle, East Cowes on 8th August 1968. When she entered service she was rostered into operations principally on direct sailings to and from East Cowes with essentially bookings for heavy vehicles.

With the new *Norris Castle* due to enter service in late 1968, it became known that the *Balmoral* was about to end her career with Red Funnel, and the last excursion of the season, scheduled for 15th September 1968, was to bring an end to the summer cruising programme for good also. Little publicity was given to the event and sadly due to inclement weather the trip was cancelled, finally ending the company's association with cruising. The ship was later chartered and eventually sold to P & A Campbell for cruising in the Bristol Channel.

Red Funnel now had four vessels maintaining their operations, with the *Norris Castle*, *Cowes Castle* and *Osborne Castle* employed all the year round, and the *Carisbrooke Castle* used during peak and overhaul periods.

The introduction of new vessels with the rival operators on the Solent, British Railways, later to be rebranded as Sealink, were to be less ambitious. This was due possibly more to the fact that the Government put restrictions on the British Railways Board over capital investment in ships during the sixties and early seventies. However, in the early seventies, the company ordered three identical sister ships, the first for Portsmouth and the other two as replacements for the Lymington operation. The first of the new ships for Lymington, the *Cenwulf*, entered service in October 1973, replacing the *Lymington*. The new class of vessels could accommodate up to 750 passengers and 52 cars. The *Cenwulf's* operating partner *Cenred* followed during January 1974 and replaced the *Farringford*.

Meanwhile, the first of the generation of this class of ships for Portsmouth, the *Cuthred* duly entered service in June 1969. She was later followed by the *Caedmon*. The introduction of these vessels now allowed Sealink to have an operational advantage over their rivals Red Funnel.

1969-1982

By 1969 Red Funnel had a fleet of four ferries on their Southampton-Cowes operation. In 1972 Red Funnel ordered a new vessel by the name of *Netley Castle*. The new double-ended ship would be able to accommodate 1,000 passengers and 80 cars. She arrived at Southampton from her builders in February 1974, but did not enter service until June due to industrial and technical troubles with the ferry. Following entering commercial operations she was to be the biggest ferry operating to the Isle of Wight services until the arrival of the *St. Catherine* in 1983. Meanwhile, the *Carisbrooke Castle* was withdrawn from service in September 1974 and later sold to Italian interests.

During September 1975, Red Funnel announced that both the *Cowes Castle* and *Norris Castle* would be sent to Rotterdam for modifications, which would include an additional 30ft to their superstructure, the height of the car deck would be raised by an additional 14ft to allow more freight to be carried, and both ships would be converted to drive-through vessels. These alterations, together with the fitting of a mezzanine deck, would increase the car capacity of both vessels to 30 cars. The *Cowes Castle* was first to be sent to Holland for modifications and returned to her home port just before Christmas. She then operated as a stern loader at Southampton, and loaded over the bow at East Cowes, with side loading taking place at West Cowes. Alterations were also made to their accommodation. Possibly one of the most distinctive changes to the vessel was the removal of the funnel further aft, to allow further open areas for passengers on the top deck. The *Norris Castle* meanwhile sailed to Rotterdam in January 1976 for similar conversion work, returning to

The **Norris Castle** pictured from the **Cowes Castle** at Southampton in March 1994. (*David Marshall)*

The ***Camber Queen*** seen here arriving at Portsmouth from Fishbourne in June 1979. *(David Marshall)*

Saturday 24th July 1965 by Mr Hugh Gordon, Sales Director of Westland Aircraft Ltd. Hovertravel's senior captain, Peter Ayles, drove the craft to Ryde and the company immediately started operations. There was no fixed timetable when the service started. Some six crossings could be made each hour in calm weather conditions. The new operation was officially inaugurated by Earl Mountbatten, the then Governor of the Isle of Wight on 4th August 1965. The quick service appealed to many on the island, especially for those working in Portsmouth. By the end of August the company had carried over 30,000 passengers. In 1966 a second hovercraft was introduced on the route.

operations during April 1976. Her passenger capacity was increased from 500 to 900 passengers.

Following the conversion of both these ferries, operations for Red Funnel were to remain on a very even keel for the next fifteen years, with the four ships maintaining operations in the summer between Southampton and East and West Cowes. In 1978, the *Osborne Castle* was sold to Canadian interests, leaving a fleet of three car ferries to maintain the forty-five minute operation.

In June 1965 a new company, Hovertravel Limited, started a new fast ferry service between Southsea and Ryde. The company established a terminal adjacent to Clarence Pier at Southsea and planning permission was granted for a slipway next to Ryde railway and coach stations at the sea front. The new operation was to work closely with the British Hovercraft Corporation when they introduced their Westland SRN6 hovercraft on the route, which were used up until 1983. A ten minute service between Clarence Pier and Ryde was introduced by Hovertravel. The first craft was handed over at East Cowes on

Their new operation offered the fastest ferry service to the island and it still operates today the fastest service to the Island. By 1969 the company had carried some one and half million passengers in four years. In 1984, two new hovercraft were introduced, which were faster and quieter and gave greater passenger comfort than the older SRN6. The new craft were also to prove far cheaper to operate.

Following the opening of the new ferry service by Hovertravel, a year later British Rail had established their own fast ferry company under the banner of Seaspeed. By the summer of 1966, the company were operating two SRN6 between Cowes and Southampton. In March 1967, a service between Cowes and Portsmouth was started. A third route, from Portsmouth to Ryde Pier, was also begun on 1st April 1968 using a larger craft which could accommodate 65 passengers. The service to Ryde was not operated by a hovercraft but by a conventionally driven fast craft with screws. The prototype craft was plagued with problems during her first season; nevertheless she was later joined by a similar sister which was placed on the Cowes-Portsmouth route. The Cowes-Portsmouth service closed in September 1969 and eventually the Southampton-Cowes service was also closed in 1976 and was taken over by Solent Seaspeed, the subsidiary of Hovertravel. A series of other craft was introduced by the company, but in the event British Rail decided not to continue their fast ferry operations as from the end of the summer season in 1976.

British Rail's Seaspeed service started in 1966 between Southampton and Cowes, was to affect the regular commuter traffic of Red Funnel and it was decided two years later that the company would start its own fast ferry service with their own fast craft. Initially the company chose the Hovermarine craft HM2 which was just coming into production. The vessel underwent trials, but due to unreliability of the first craft then operating for Seaspeed on the Solent, the whole operation was cancelled by Red Funnel.

Following the misfortune of their first planned fast ferry service, the company decided to order a Seaflight 857 hydrofoil to commence operations as from 1969. The Italian-built craft was able to carry 54 passengers and operate at a service speed between 37 and 40 m.p.h. The first vessel, named *Shearwater*, duly entered service in May 1969. A series of further hydrofoils were duly purchased or chartered during the next twelve years, including two hovercraft which were acquired in 1981 for two seasons. By May 1982, the company had brought up their fleet of hydrofoils to four vessels maintaining

Red Funnel's ***Netley Castle*** will be replaced by a third sister to the ***Red Falcon*** during 1996. *(Miles Cowsill)*

the Southampton-West Cowes service.

1982-1995

Meanwhile, the continued growth in car traffic to the Isle of Wight in the early eighties brought further expansion plans by the Sealink. Capacity and congestion problems at their Portsmouth Broad Street terminal were solved when they purchased the now redundant Gunwharf site, adjacent to the existing terminal at Broad Street. The site was cleared and a new well appointed terminal with large parking facilities was duly constructed and opened on 21st February 1982. Meanwhile, in September 1981, Sealink unveiled plans for a similar expansion and improvements at Fishbourne.

Sealink also ordered two new car ferries for the Portsmouth-Fishbourne service at a cost of £5 million each. The first vessel, named *St. Catherine*, was duly launched on 30th March 1983 and arrived the following June at Portsmouth, entering service on 3rd July 1983 as the largest car ferry ever to be built for the Isle of Wight services with a length of 250ft. The new generation of car

Traditional travel meets the era of fast ferry service on the Solent. The elegant ***Southsea*** seen here passing ***Our Lady Patricia*** in June 1986. *(Maritime Photographic)*

ferries offered a far greater standard of luxury than the previous vessels on the route, and also offered increased capacity with space for 142 cars on two deck levels and 1,000 passengers. With the mezzanine deck raised, the vessel could handle 24 commercial vehicles. Following her entry into service, the *Fishbourne* was withdrawn from service. The second ship, the *St. Helen*, was launched in September and arrived in Portsmouth on 24th November. On the arrival of the *St. Helen* she replaced the *Caedmon* which was switched to Lymington to operate with her sisters. Meanwhile, the *Cuthred* was retained for summer work on the link.

In July 1984, Sealink was privatised and purchased by Sea Containers for £66 million. A new livery and name of Sealink British Ferries was introduced as a result of the purchase of the the former railway company.

Meanwhile, the third sister in the 'Saint' class series was duly ordered and the *St. Cecilia* arrived at Portsmouth in March 1987. A fourth vessel, the *St. Faith* was later ordered by Sealink British Ferries in 1989 for the Portsmouth-Fishbourne link. All four sister ships were to prove an overwhelming success and were to grow the market for the company.

Sealink British Ferries returned to the fast ferry market in 1985 when it was announced by the Bermuda-based Sea Containers that two fast craft would be ordered from International Catamarans of Hobart, Tasmania for the Portsmouth-Ryde operation. Each fast craft would cost £1.9 million and would be able to carry 470 passengers across Spithead in 15 minutes. The first of the fast 'Cat' craft, *Our Lady Patricia*, arrived at Portsmouth on 29th March. The second craft, *Our Lady Pamela*, was delivered some four months later and took up service on 9th August. The new fast ferries were to prove successful but were the end of the traditional and classic ferry travel between both ports of the Denny built vessels.

The *Shanklin* was first to be disposed of by the company, the *Brading* was eventually retired and offered for sale but sadly ended her days at the breakers' yard at Portsmouth in 1994. Meanwhile, the *Southsea* continued as a relief vessel to the fast ferry operation in the summer until the end of the 1988 season. She still remains in the ownership of Sea Containers, having been laid up at Newhaven for many years with an uncertain future.

Plans to improve the terminal facilities at Lymington and to introduce new vessels on the service have been thwarted to date. The company as early as 1989 had drawn up plans for improvements to Lymington Harbour and to introduce new vessels of a standard operating on the Portsmouth-Fishbourne route.

In spring 1990, Sealink British Ferries was acquired by the Swedish ferry company Stena Line. As part of the takeover bid, the Isle of Wight services were excluded and remained under the ownership of Sea Containers. A new company brand name, Wightlink, was duly launched in November 1990 for future operations.

In the light of the major investment and rapid improvement in the Fishbourne-Ryde service by Sealink and later Wightlink, Red Funnel were left with an ageing fleet, which was now no match to that of either the Portsmouth or Lymington services. In the sixties the company had been ahead of their rivals, and major capital investment was now required for new tonnage.

Red Funnel were acquired by Associated British Ports in 1989, which was to prove a valuable move for the established operation.

The **St.Helen** and **Normandie** captured on a brisk August afternoon outward bound from Portsmouth. *(Miles Cowsill)*

The takeover was to allow Red Funnel to order vital new tonnage to compete with their competitors. Two new high-speed passenger craft appeared in 1991, to be followed the next year by the first of two new car ferries.

The launch of the ***Red Falcon*** on the Clyde. *(Red Funnel)*

Red Funnel introduced two new fast craft during 1991, firstly the *Redjet 1* on 11th April, and then *Redjet 2* some three months later. The new craft were able to achieve a speed of 32.5 knots and able to carry 120 passengers. Their entry into service enabled the company to offer a half-hourly service to West Cowes. In the meantime, the company decided to concentrate all their car ferry operations on East Cowes, instead of splitting their services between West and East Cowes. The reason given for the reorganisation of the sailings of the car ferries was to increase the schedules between Southampton and East Cowes to 18 sailings every week day, and it would enable them to run an hourly service between 04.00 and 23.00.

Meanwhile, during the late summer in 1992, Red Funnel ordered the first of their two new double-decked ended car ferries for their Southampton-East Cowes route. The first of the vessels was due for delivery during 1994 and the second during the latter part of the year. Both new ships, built in Glasgow, would eventually replace the *Cowes Castle* and *Norris Castle* and would have a capacity for 140 cars and 700 passengers.

The first of the new ferries for Red Funnel arrived on 1st March 1994 at Southampton in the new company's livery. The *Red Falcon* now allowed the company to compete with Wightlink with coach traffic, something they had not been able to do until her arrival. With a service speed of 14 knots on the 55-minute service the 'Falcon' offered a new era and standards for the company.

On entry into service of the *Red Falcon*, the *Cowes Castle* was withdrawn from service and sold to Croatian interests. Meanwhile, the second new ferry, *Red Osprey* entered service on 21st October, this allowed the *Norris Castle* to be disposed of, again to the same Croatian ferry company.

It had been originally planned that the *Netley Castle* would undergo a major refit during the winter of 1994/95 to bring her accommodation up to a similar standard to that of the new ferries. In the event, the company decided to order a third new vessel to replace the *Netley Castle* for delivery in 1996. On the entry into service of the third vessel, it will be the first time in the history of Red Funnel that they will have three nearly identical car ferries.

Red Funnel were to see an increase in their market share from 18% to 21% following the introduction of the *Red Osprey* on the Isle of Wight services. The entry into service was also to see an aggressive marketing campaign by the company to improve on these figures, prior to the arrival of the third new ferry, which will be slightly larger than her sisters.

Meanwhile, fast ferry operations to West Cowes are still operated by the Red Jets catamarans and hydrofoils.

There have been other rival operations on the Solent, possibly the most recent competitor Cowes Express is worthy of note. This company started operating from Southampton to Cowes in 1992, initially with two craft, the *Wight King* and *Wight Prince*. Initially the company offered a cheaper fare structure to that of Red Funnel and they also planned to take on their other rivals on the Solent, Wightlink, at a later stage. In the event these plans were to come to nothing and the company folded in 1993.

Today the Solent is served by a relatively modern fleet of ferries operating an efficient ferry service to the island. Wightlink continues to consider feasibility plans to improve the Lymington-Yarmouth service with new tonnage and harbour facilities at Lymington. It is hoped that in the near future the differences between the company and those involved in the protection of Lymington harbour can be resolved so that Wightlink can introduce new tonnage to compete with the other services to the island. Failure to agree the terms could possibly see the demise of this route in the long term.

The **Red Falcon** and **Red Osprey** pictured together in Southampton Water. *(Red Funnel)*

SEA DOUBLE

55 minute cruise Southampton to East Cowes.

Having the most luxurious ship on the Solent wasn't enough for Red Funnel. Now, we have the two most luxurious ships on the Solent.

Double the comfort! Twice the number of bars and cafes serving hot and cold food. And a twofold increase in sun decks!

The launch of Red Osprey means our passengers are pampered on almost every crossing.

A relaxed wander around will soon convince you of our commitment to excellence in our service.

Our crew are, as ever, attentive and courteous. Indeed, in every aspect on board we've endeavoured to make every crossing like a cruise.

However you choose to travel, on foot, by car or by coach, we're sure you'll enjoy being aboard our new flagships.

For those of you who have to dash, the quick option is to take a Red Jet. You'll barely have time to settle into your comfortable seat. Just a 22 minute skim across the water and you're there!

FOR RESERVATIONS
TELEPHONE
SOUTHAMPTON: 01703 330333.

HUGE INVESTMENT GIVES RED FUNNEL A COMPETITIVE EDGE

In 1989, Associated British Ports (ABP), owners of the port of Southampton and other ports around the country, acquired the Southampton/Isle of Wight operator, Red Funnel Ferries, a company with a proud history going back to 1861.

Over the last five years ABP has amply demonstrated its faith in the Isle of Wight as a long-term holiday destination and its commitment to the 130,000 inhabitants of Britain's 'Garden Island' by instituting a major programme of investment in all sectors of Red Funnel.

Two Hi-Speed passenger catamarans were purchased in 1990, and in 1992 orders were placed for two new high capacity ro-ro ferries. These were built on the Clyde in Scotland and came into service during 1994. A third sister ship, with larger passenger accommodation, was ordered in 1994 to be delivered to Southampton prior to the commencement of the 1996 summer season.

The design brief was simple - to provide ships of sufficient size to cater for modern traffic loads and to offer the travelling public facilities and comfort never before experienced on a short haul ferry service of this type.

Journey time between Southampton and our Island port of East Cowes is just under the hour - sufficient duration for our customers to enjoy a bite to eat, a drink at the bar and wander around the sun deck.

In fact, bar the odd winter gale, the journey to and from the Isle of Wight is a pleasant cruise all the year round and our

Alistair Whyte

two new ships, *Red Falcon* and *Red Osprey,* capitalise on that, making the voyage part of the holiday experience.

By achieving that, we are in some ways stepping back in history, for a trip to the Isle of Wight in the 1860s when the Southampton, Isle of Wight and South of England Royal Mail Steam Packet Company Limited was formed, was considered more of an adventure than going to France today.

Queen Victoria is credited as being one of those who put the island on the map as a holiday resort among high society, when yacht racing at Cowes was for the truly élite.

Red Funnel grew considerably in the latter part of the century and between the wars, and as well as scheduled services to the island, offered a variety of summer excursions, including day trips to Cherbourg, before hostilities again broke out in 1939.

But it was during the 1960s and early 1970s that tourism hit its peak, and Red Funnel responded with the introduction of its 'Castle' class ships which were the company's first purpose, designed vehicle/passenger ferries rather than passenger ferries which carried a few vehicles.

Although vehicle traffic has continued to grow to the Isle of Wight, its honeymoon period as a top holiday resort ended as the more adventurous British discovered cheap package holidays to Europe's sunspots, particularly Spain.

However, there is a hint of the fashion business about holidays and there is strong evidence that the Isle of Wight is again back on the list of many British people as a clean and relatively unspoilt holiday spot which combines a good climate with a slower pace of life not found elsewhere on the south coast within such easy reach of London and the Midlands.

A strong Isle of Wight tourism business is essential to the ferry operators and Red Funnel has helped to generate extra traffic through its Sailaway Holidays and Short Breaks brochure launched in 1993 which offers a full range of hotel, self catering and holiday centre packages from two, three and four day breaks to the traditional summer fortnight.

Coupled with our involvement in the Isle of Wight Image Campaign, these initiatives have seen the Isle of Wight bucking the general downwards trend in British holiday bookings in 1994.

With a bigger and better Image Campaign in 1995, the message will go still further afield, hopefully generating larger numbers of visitors, some renewing a childhood acquaintance and others making the trip across the Solent for the first time.

We strongly believe we have to offer a service beyond that which the customer expects, whether it be the once a year holidaymaker, the commuter or the truck or coach driver.

One of the first things to happen at Red Funnel following the change of ownership was the introduction of a timetable which provided a much improved service for our customers.

Red Funnel used to be regarded as the service that shut down at 7pm or 8pm, and even though our new timetable has been in operation for several years, a reputation like that is hard to shake off.

In the winter months we run a last ferry sailing at 10pm from Southampton and 11.15pm from East Cowes, while on Friday and Saturdays in the summer we run an 11pm service from Southampton with a quarter past midnight return from the Island.

In the mornings, the first service from Southampton is at 4am and at 4.30am during the winter. We are conscious that freight operators in particular find it beneficial to travel at night and it may be necessary to run additional sailings to suit these customers.

The second element we set out to improve was the Hi-Speed service between Southampton and West Cowes, with initially an easier to remember timetable and then the first fruits of investment in the form of two Red Jet catamarans, each with a passenger capacity of 130.

These craft, which were built on the Isle of Wight, have improved the comfort factor and the reliability of the service, particularly in the winter. They are able to handle more adverse weather conditions than the Shearwater hydrofoils and can also operate effectively in thick fog.

Revamped terminal facilities in West Cowes and a brand new Hi-Speed terminal at Town Quay, Southampton, complete the executive touches that have seen Red Funnel increase its market share to nudging 30% in this sector.

The big challenge to the new Red Funnel of the early 1990s was the car ferry fleet - which, though well maintained and in good seaworthy order, offered outdated freight and passenger facilities.

The *Cowes Castle* and *Norris Castle* belonged to the pre-container transport age when a 15 tonner was a good sized truck and cars were taller and narrower.

Even so, we were able to demonstrate that despite the limitations imposed by these elderly vessels, we could boost our market share, and that gave us the confidence to grasp the nettle and order replacements for the *Cowes Castle* and *Norris Castle* which had both seen in excess of 25 years service.

That confidence has been borne out by *Red Falcon*, the first of the new Raptor class ferries, which entered service on the Southampton-East Cowes route during the week before Easter 1994.

From that time to the end of September, Red Funnel's share of the car ferry travel market rose from 18% to 21% and with the introduction of *Red Osprey* in October 1994, we have a solid platform for 1995 when we are expecting to make further gains in all sectors of the market.

The huge £24 million investment will be completed in the early months of 1996 when the third of the Raptor class designs joins the fleet, giving us the most modern and the safest ships on the Solent.

Certainly the last five years has been one of the most active periods in the 134 years history of Red Funnel, and we have by no means finished yet.

Red Funnel's ***Red Jet 2*** pictured at Southampton. *(David Marshall)*

Terminal facilities in Southampton will be one of the issues to be addressed over the next five years together with further improvements in the Hi-Speed service.

Our investment has not only been in machinery and equipment but in people, and we are determined to continue to provide the training which gives our front line staff the knowledge and confidence to deal effectively with problems as they arise.

What the ABP purchase of Red Funnel has done is to give the company a clear sense of direction. It is now a strong and credible competitor on the Island route with a determination to supply the best service on the most sophisticated vessels on the Solent.

Alistair Whyte
Managing Director
Red Funnel Group

MORE CROSSINGS TO THE ISLE OF WIGHT

All these convenient routes are yours when you sail with Wightlink: Lymington-Yarmouth, Portsmouth - Fishbourne (24 hrs) and Portsmouth Harbour - Ryde.

Wightlink not only crosses more frequently but offers you comfort and style, and first class service as standard.

Short breaks are also available all year round, as we have the largest range of ferry inclusive package holidays to the island.

So, if you would like more crossings to more destinations, staff that are keen to please and a service that never sleeps, ring 01705 827744 for enquiries and car bookings now.

GET THE *link*

UP TO 87 CROSSINGS, 24 HOURS A DAY. IF YOU GET THE LINK.

WITH QUALITY SERVICE WE WILL EXCELL

Many people are surprised to learn that Wightlink, with its predecessors, have been operating ferry services to the Isle of Wight for over 160 years! In 1994 we carried some 5 million passengers, nearly 1 million cars and some 250,000 coaches and freight lorries on our three routes to the Island. With nine ships in our fleet and a revenue of some £36 million per annum, it is a large and important business.

The first ferry services went from the Port of Lymington and called at Portsmouth before crossing to Ryde, Cowes and eventually Yarmouth on the Isle of Wight. In the 1830's the poor road systems encouraged people to travel by sea between Lymington, a beautiful port in the New Forest area, and Portsmouth. Although road systems are now very well developed, some may argue that peak hour traffic on the M27 and M275 causes similar comparisons!

The Isle of Wight captures wonderfully the spirit of Olde England with many countryside, village and beach areas that stand as a comparison with anywhere in the UK. Accommodation is mostly made up of small hotels and guest houses, which gives the opportunity of a truly personal service to visitors. There are also many attractions from historic sites (including the oldest dinosaur bones in the UK), to wonderful houses (such as Osborne House, a residence of Queen Victoria) and outdoor attractions (such as Blackgang Chine and the Steam Railway).

Despite these advantages, the Isle of Wight has suffered over recent years from a decline in the number of visitors. The attraction of package holidays to overseas destinations has drawn a larger proportion of UK holidaymakers. In 1994, the island, strongly supported by Wightlink, started an image campaign to influence UK holidaymakers considering their next holiday. In particular, the Isle of Wight offers fantastic facilities for short break visits.

Mel Williams

Positive results from this campaign brought growth to the visitors market of some 5%, reversing the decline evident since 1989. Continuation of this campaign, together with improvements in the facilities and infrastructure of the island, will continue to bring positive growth in island visitors into the future.

Wightlink operates three ships for passengers and vehicles between Lymington and Yarmouth on the island. This is the most picturesque route and the journey takes only 30 minutes. It is a very important link between the beauty of the New Forest and the quieter western side of the Isle of Wight.

Two routes operate from Portsmouth. Our passenger-only service links the rail heads of Portsmouth Harbour and Ryde Pier using 400 seater catamarans. The other route sees our four largest 'Saint Class ships connecting Portsmouth Gunwharf and Fishbourne. This is the only Island service which operates 24 hours a day and 365 days of the year.

Vehicle ferries offer excellent, high standards of customer facilities, with on-board bar & buffet and comfortable, spacious lounge areas. On the Portsmouth to Fishbourne route, there are lifts from the car decks to the lounge, and 1994 saw the introduction of electronic information screens on this route's terminals. 1994 also saw over half a million pounds invested in the refurbishment of Portsmouth Harbour terminal, which now offers foot passengers an efficient, modern and comfortable facility. It is intended to invest similarly in a refurbishment programme for Ryde Pier Head terminal in 1995.

The flexibility of the Portsmouth routes and the good motorway connections to the city mean that significant future growth will be absorbed by these services. Significant investment in our Portsmouth facilities and the wider opportunities of connecting with longer sea routes out of the city add significant potential.

Growth in current services and opportunities to develop new routes will mean that Wightlink will be around for at least another 150 years! Our great experience of operating quality services to the island offers a strong platform to achieve future success, and the 600 staff of Wightlink, many of them residents of the island, are the most important asset the company has to achieve continuing success from a base of excellent customer service.

Mel Williams
Managing Director, Wightlink

Maritime Portsmouth. From left to right, the Royal Yacht ***Britannia***, Wightlink's ***St. Faith, St. Helen*** and ***Our Lady Pamela***. In the background, the historical vessels ***HMS Warrior*** and ***HMS Victory*** can be seen. *(Maritime Photographic)*

STILL THE FASTEST

Hovertravel was started in 1965 by a number of brave individuals with aviation, civil engineering and financial backgrounds. The enterprise represented the world's first year-round hovercraft service and made use of the hovercraft's main attribute; as a natural amphibian it could traverse land and water. The Ryde-Southsea route was in many ways ideal, a tidal four mile stretch of water separating two comparatively densely populated areas where incomes were such that they could support fast transport. At low tide half a mile of sand separated Ryde from the waters edge - the hovercraft averaged 9 minutes for the journey between Ryde Esplanade and Southsea Green.

The Ryde-Portsmouth route had been pioneered by the Railway Companies. In 1865 they ran 10 knot paddle steamers to connect the Isle of Wight and mainland railheads. This involved enormously expensive piers which were built at Portsmouth and Ryde to enable the boats to dock at all states of tide. Had the hovercraft appeared one hundred years earlier the piers would never have been built.

Hovertravel started with two leased 38 seater SRN6 hovercraft manufactured by Saunders Row of Cowes. As the route became more popular these were replaced with larger and larger machines culminating in today's 100 seaters which shuttle backwards and forwards on a fifteen minute schedule. Originally the hovercraft cost twice as much as the existing boats - ten shillings. Today, due to enormous strides in design and thereby efficiency the hovercraft is the same price and in some cases cheaper than the displacement

The ***Freedom 90*** arriving at Ryde *(Miles Cowsill)*

vessels it competes with.

The first day the hovercraft was introduced as a public service 800 people were carried, this was on July 24th 1965. Since this time over 14,000,000 have made the four mile trip together with hundreds of tons of parcels and a large proportion of the Isle of Wight's mail.

Hovertravel manufacture their hovercraft in partnership with Westland Aircraft, who took over Saunders Row in the 1960's, at a modern facility at St. Helens on the Isle of Wight. In the past they have operated in many parts of the world doing what the hovercraft does best - providing a fast fully amphibious platform for various types of mineral survey work in areas of the globe where conventional boats go aground and wheeled or tracked vehicles sink.

Hovertravel has had a long association with Portsmouth famous for all types of marine transport stretching back many centuries. Hover travel now represents the only hovercraft service available to the public within the British Isles. Plans for continued expansion abound.

C. D. J. Bland
Managing Director, Hovertravel.

LITTLE FERRIES AND SOLENT VISITORS

The scope required of this chapter is very wide ranging. It is impossible to do justice to every operator and every vessel that could, justifiably, be included. The writer has, therefore, had to be highly selective, choosing to give a recent historical perspective and to highlight vessels of particular interest, even if their fame arises from areas outside the Solent (e.g. the *Waverley* and the *Bournemouth Queen*). As far as is possible, he tries to journey from east to west, though many operators spread their cruises far and wide.

Certainly, what can now be considered as the joyous days of pleasure cruising in post-war cruising, in the 1950's, when South Parade Pier and Clarence Pier, both on Southsea's seafront, and the Royal Pier at Southampton catered for the regular comings and goings of pleasure craft ranging from small, open launches to large paddle steamers like the *Ryde*, the *Sandown* and the *Princess Elizabeth*, are now well and truly gone. Yet, there are some encouraging signs, notably in the use of smaller vessels and the story of Wightline Cruises bears that out. The effects of the recession are keenly felt by all operators; hopefully, their futures will blossom and the passenger numbers on their cruises and ferry routes will increase in the years to come.

Operating the largest of the "small" boats is the Gosport Ferry Company Ltd. which maintains the link between Portsmouth and Gosport. The company had been known as the Portsmouth Harbour Ferry Company until recently, but the change in nomenclature reflects the

The ***Island Rose*** arriving at Yarmouth *(John Hendy)*

name given to it by generations of commuters and trippers on both waterfronts.

The origins of the company can be traced back to the 1870's when the first of many steam-powered launches made her appearance. There were originally two, quite separate, companies at first competing on the route and then, later, coming to an amicable working agreement, sharing the service between them. The grey-funnelled launches had names beginning with the prefix "Ferry" and belonged to the Gosport and Portsea Watermen's Steam Launch Company; the *Ferry Belle* (of 1924) is a typical example. The other concern was the Port of Portsmouth Steam Launch and Towing Company whose distinguishing mark was cream funnels. Their vessels had names beginning with the letter "V", one of which, the *Vadne* (of 1939) still exists as a hulk, used as a floating platform in Weevil Creek, Gosport.

There was a third operator, the Floating Bridge Company, which, unfortunately ceased trading in the late 1950's. As well as operating floating bridges from The Point, Old Portsmouth, it also had pleasure vessels not unlike those of the other two concerns. Their last steam launch was the *Princessa* (of 1921; see below) which served the company until its end, when she was sold to Southampton's Blue Funnel Company and was later converted to diesel operation by them. Towards the end of her steam days, she sank in a storm off Ryde Pier when lying at her overnight mooring. The *Princessa* is now to be found at Falmouth where she operates river cruises and sports a rather garish colour scheme.

The last of the steam launches left Portsmouth Harbour in 1968. By then with her funnel painted in the rather rich bluey-green of the amalgamated company (formed in 1961), the 1948-built *Ferry Princess* departed for service on the River Thames, serving in the Charing Cross to Greenwich reaches of the capital's river. Near-sister *Venus* (also 1948) was sold locally to Blue Funnel. Both were subsequently converted to diesel operation, although the *Venus* is now believed to be a sailing vessel somewhere in the region of Australia. At the time of writing, the *Ferry Princess* has been lying on a slipway for some months at Blackwall.

Maintaining the tradition of the continuous, open-deck design (with small, dimly-lit saloons below the waterline), three diesel vessels appeared on the Gosport route. The *Vesta* came first in 1956, followed by the *Ferry Queen* in 1959 and, finally, the *Vita* in 1960. Their superstructure was far from identical and so they were easily distinguishable. All three were employed in a cruising capacity, as well as fulfilling their cross-harbour duties. However, on balance the *Vita* spent rather more time on the ferry route than *Vesta* which was frequently to be seen cruising along Southsea seafront (from South Parade Pier) on Portsmouth Harbour trips. On Tuesday, 31st October, 1967, the *Ferry Queen* braved somewhat lumpy seas to join a flotilla of ships escorting the famous Cunarder, *Queen Mary*, on her final departure, as she sailed to Long Beach, California.

In 1974, all three of these vessels made their way to the nation's capital; *Ferry Queen* and *Vita* are still operating on the Thames. However, the *Vesta,* having been renamed *Duchess M*, has subsequently moved north to the Tyne. These little ferries were old before their time; after all, their basic design went back eighty years! Crossing the harbour on a cold, sometimes foggy, winter's evening, with dozens of bicycles (belonging to dockyard workers, commuting from Gosport) seemingly entangled on the foredeck was not the first choice of any but the hardened enthusiast. The lack of radar occasionally caused somewhat elongated journeys and one or two "hairy" moments!

By contrast, the two vessels built in 1966 were years, if not decades, ahead of their time. Described as something more akin to Hong Kong, the futuristic-looking *Portsmouth Queen* and *Gosport Queen* were launched in tandem. With their wheelhouses offset to port and seating accommodation on the main and promenade decks only on the starboard side (save at either end), there is a large, empty space along their port length for bicycles and motorcycles. With two funnels, of unequal height, and the ability to move sideways, they were referred to as "crabs" and, indeed, did shake considerably the notion of what a ferry should look like.

It says much for the company's forward thinking that the two vessels are approaching their thirtieth birthdays, still giving sterling service as the main craft on the route. Given the short time that it takes to cross the harbour - about five minutes - luxury seating is not required, and it is difficult to conceive of any vessel better equipped for the service.

A slightly larger cruise vessel, the *Gay Enterprise*, entered service in 1971. Her real purpose was to provide support on the ferry route when one or other of the Queens is on refit. Yet she spends most of her time cruising and undertakes some charter work. When ferrying, she is stripped of her more luxurious fittings which are quickly re-instated when she resumes her more glamorous role. The *Gay Enterprise* received the more appropriate name of *Solent Enterprise* in 1979.

A fourth, but smaller version of the new generation of ferries, appeared in 1974. This was the *Southsea Queen*. Of marginally more traditional design - she has a pointed bow, as opposed to the rounded prows of the larger vessels - she was not so successful as her consorts and trade proved insufficient for the company to employ her beyond 1978 when she moved to Southampton Water and trades under the name of *Hythe Hotspur*.

For many years, the three ships have sported apple-green and white liveries. The *Solent Enterprise* has been adorned with an extra band, originally red but, latterly, dark green. The two Queens have carried the distinctive motif, "It's shorter by water!"

Like many ferry operators, the company has had to witness the decline of passenger numbers. The diminishing in size of the workforce in Portsmouth dockyard has decreased cross-harbour traffic. Furthermore, a motorway network has sprung around the east and north of the harbour, so encouraging the use of the private car.

In the 1950's and early 1960's, four vessels maintained the route throughout most of the working day. The provision of the larger Queens replaced this diagram with just the two craft. Now, only between 0630 and 0930 hours and 1530 to 1830 hours is there a two-ship service on weekdays, though Saturdays usually require this frequency. During Navy Days, one of the Queens is to be found operating into the naval base from Gosport, providing a longer and more interesting journey. The

A packed **Portsmouth Queen** on her way across Portsmouth Harbour in August 1994. *(Miles Cowsill)*

Solent Enterprise has also been chartered to Wightlink and has relieved on the Portsmouth-Ryde ferry route when necessary.

Passenger certification has changed. Following passenger shipping disasters elsewhere, the Queens' maximum passenger carrying capacity has been reduced from 500 to 300 and, in 1966, will be further reduced to 250. Similarly, the *Solent Enterprise's* passenger complement has been reduced by 50 to 250. The reasons for these reductions are primarily financial; although having a fine safety record, the Gosport Ferry Company has to comply with new legislation requiring additional safety equipment. As the vessels are rarely full, it makes more economic sense simply to decrease the maximum passenger capacity.

In addition to the ferry route, harbour tours are operated for as long each year as there is a market. Charters occur when the *Solent Enterprise* may visit unlikely places such as Yarmouth, Southampton and Beaulieu, but her more usual ports of call are Ryde and Cowes, once she is beyond the Portsmouth area. She has the certification to allow her to go south of the Isle of Wight to Sandown, but, at present, there is no demand for that. Similarly, it is possible for the Queens to operate in the Solent but this is rarely, if ever, necessary.

The company has a working relationship with two smaller concerns, namely those of J. Butcher (whose blue launches carry the suffix James in their names) and M. Pearce. The latter has two rather elderly craft, the *Darthula II* (of 1939) and the *Folkestone Belle* (of 1928). For some years of her existence, the *Folkestone Belle* carried the name of *Southsea Belle* but the original was re-instated when her Dunkerque connections became more commonly known. The Gosport company's two launches, *Solent Prince* and *Solent Princess*, are also smartly attired in a blue livery.

On the eastern flank of Portsmouth, at Eastney, is to be found a small red-hulled vessel, looking rather like a pram. This is the *Pride of Hayling* (1989) which operates an efficient and frequent service to Hayling Island. Her route takes her across the mouth of Langstone Harbour and her journey time is only about three minutes. A variety of vessels has undertaken the route over the years and names such as *Tarpon* and *Sinah* were familiar in the 1950's and 1960's. Indeed, the *Folkestone Belle* is believed to have done service on this route.

Some miles west of Portsmouth Harbour is to be found Southampton Water, and it is here that we find a comparable ferry service to that of the Gosport ferry. The route is from the recently refurbished and considerably upgraded Southampton Town Quay to Hythe Pier, along which a narrow gauge railway operates.

Records trace the route back to Elizabethan days, but a most interesting fact concerns the wooden paddle steamer, *Emerald* (of 1830). Constructed for a new company, led by Mr. W. C. Westlake, the vessel operated a daily return trip from Southampton to Cowes, Isle of Wight in addition to her Southampton-Hythe duties. Mr. Westlake was also prone to take on towage work and even occasional excursions, using the *Emerald*, much to the inconvenience and annoyance of Hythe passengers. By 1832, the little ship was taken off the route and used almost exclusively on the longer Isle of Wight

The former Red Funnel vessel ***Balmoral*** pictured at Newport, Isle of Wight in June 1992. *(David Marshall)*

The Southampton-Hythe ferry ***Hotspur IV*** pictured at Southampton in August 1994.
(Miles Cowsill)

service, being sold to the forerunners of the present Red Funnel Company in 1833.

The route developed in the nineteenth century from the use of wherries to specially constructed ferries and launches. Some were charming little paddle steamers, such as the *Hampton* (of 1894). Significantly, the name *Hotspur* came into existence when the 1899 paddler of this name first appeared. A special feature of these ships was the full length sponsons, an unusual characteristic which is still evident today, on the screw-propelled *Hotspur IV*.

The *Hotspur II*, a twin-screw diesel vessel, joined the route in 1936. The company, General Estates, then ordered *Hotspur III*, a little larger than her near sister, and this first operated in 1938. It was not until after the Second World War, that *Hotspur IV* entered service, making her presence known in 1946. This vessel replaced the ageing *Hotspur*.

The three Hotspurs were in a unique position to view the great liners entering and leaving Southampton, frequently referred to as "the gateway to the world". A highlight for passengers came on 25th April, 1961, when the six years old, 608 feet long Cunard *Ivernia*, grounded only a matter of yards from Hythe Pier. The liner was en route to Canada.

In 1968, the *Hotspur IV* lost her funnel in favour of slender, twin uptakes, when she was recommissioned with new diesel engines. The following year, the *Hotspur III* was also fitted with new diesels, but she, fortunately, retained her funnel.

An order was placed with Marine Services, Hythe, in autumn, 1977, for a new ferry to replace the *Hotspur II*. However the shipyard proprietors went into liquidation in December of that year.

In April, 1978, the General Estates Company put in a bid for Gosport's *Southsea Queen* (see above); this was successful and she began her Hythe commitment in July. Her name was changed to *Hythe Hotspur* on the 25th September. A quick repainting had replaced her previous green livery by white. Her accommodation was suitably upgraded.

The *Hythe Hotspur* was primarily the cruise ship, only operating on the Southampton Water passage when either *Hotspur III* or *Hotspur IV* was unavailable. This second-hand vessel released the *Hotspur II* for sale and she took up new duties on the Clyde in March 1979, under the name of *Kenilworth*.

Two years later, a dry inspection of the hull revealed that *Hotspur III*, by then forty-two years old, had suffered major deterioration. She was demolished in February/March 1981, having been withdrawn from service after her final passage on 13th October, 1980. Her demolition took place on the mud, near the pier she had served so faithfully for so long.

The engines of the *Hotspur II* were to be used as the propulsion for a new vessel to be built at Littlehampton, Sussex. The *New Forester*, breaking the long tradition of Hotspur names, but, nonetheless, recalling an earlier vessel of 1836 (called the *Forester*), began service on 29th August, 1982. This craft marked a significant change in the concept of the Hythe ferry; she is constructed more on the modern greenhouse, motor bus principle.

After approximately 100 years of ownership, General Estates sold, the route to Derek Shipping Ltd. in 1991, who chartered all three vessels to maintain the route. In November, 1993, this company went into liquidation and, until the 8th January, 1994, Hampshire County Council provided a service through the liquidator. The current operators, White Horse Ferries, then took on the route, purchasing the *Hotspur IV* from General Estates whilst taking on the *New Forester* on charter. The pier at Hythe was included in the purchase, but *Hythe Hotspur* was not, still being owned by General Estates. Hence, in summer 1994, this vessel was available to undertake charter work for Blue Funnel.

White Horse Ferries Ltd. is known for the Tilbury to Gravesend route, which they took over in March, 1991. Within months, they had replaced the traditional ferry with a purpose-built catamaran, the sixty-seven feet long *Great Expectations*, with a passenger capacity for ninety-five. She was constructed on the former railway pier at Gravesend. At the time of writing, October 1994, White Horse is giving serious consideration to the transfer of this craft to the Southampton-Hythe link, replacing her on the River Thames with a new vessel of similar type. The *Great Expectations* will have to operate at a considerably slower speed in Southampton Water, owing to local restrictions.

It is intended to keep the *Hotspur IV* as a support ferry and also to use her on cruise and charter work. This is most encouraging, as, approaching her fiftieth birthday, the ship is much appreciated by nostalgia-minded enthusiasts and, indeed, by regular commuters on the route.

Just as the Gosport ferries (for which an unsuccessful bid was made in 1994) have changed colours over the years, so have these vessels. The original colour scheme applied to *Hotspur* in 1889 was a black hull and a black funnel, with a white band being added to the latter shortly afterwards. This remained until April, 1963, when General Estates announced their decision to experiment with a blue and cream livery on the *Hotspur IV*. Proving successful, a similar scheme was applied to the *Hotspur II* and the *Hotspur III*, although a slightly darker blue was chosen. Variations on this theme appeared over the years. In recent times, an attractive maroon hull, white upperworks and a rich buff funnel emerged, but on becoming Waterfront Ferries (Derek Shipping's trading name), navy blue and white became the norm. This has been maintained by White Horse, though bright red and white may well replace this; these colours have already replaced this on one of the train carriages on Hythe Pier.

The Blue Funnel Company, now based at the Ocean Village, Southampton, for many years operated a fleet of former Gosport ferries. The *Princessa* and the *Venus* were fleetmates of Blue Funnel's *Varos*, *Verda*, *Ferry King* (renamed *Solent Queen*) and *Sandringham*. All these steamers were gradually converted to diesel operation and acquired dummy funnels, the effect of which was spoilt by it being possible to see through the new deckhouses immediately underneath. Nonetheless, they had a most attractive profile, as robust little cruising ships.

Sadly, many of these vessels no longer exist, or, if they do, their whereabouts are unknown. The *Sandringham* lived out her final days as a floating platform on the river bank in Southampton for many years. The *Verda* changed hands more than once. After lying in a rather sorry state at Newhaven for some time, she was purchased by new owners and moved to Shoreham a couple of years ago. She has now sunk at her moorings. The *Princessa* was the last of the former Gosport "liners" to grace this fleet.

The first purpose-built vessel was the *Solent Scene*. Slightly larger than the former Gosport fleet, she has more enclosed accommodation and features better facilities generally. Three years later, in 1977, her near-sister appeared in the form of the *Island Scene*. These ships, originally all-over white, save for the funnel, now sport navy blue hulls with white upperworks, so improving their appearance. Over the years, differences between them have emerged. The most obvious is the *Island Scene's* fully enclosed stern, which, unfortunately, has given her a rather box-like appearance when viewed from certain angles.

Blue Funnel was quick to realise that its future depended upon a wider market that just cruising around Southampton, Beaulieu, the River Hamble, and Solent confines. Indeed, its principal commitment to cruising was largely based on the wide assortment of liners arriving at and leaving from the docks at Southampton. This was now sadly diminished, with only a handful of large, attractive liners in the form of the *Queen Elizabeth 2*, *Canberra*, and *Achille Lauro*, to mention three of the most striking.

Thus, it was appropriate to order a function ship, which could cruise and yet be a floating dance hall, restaurant, discotheque, grandstand for firework displays and so on. Although a monohulled vessel, the *Leisure Scene* (1985) is very broadly beamed and so is ideally designed to fulfil these requirements.

In 1994, a further new ship arrived in

the fleet; she is the *Ocean Scene*. A development of the principles underlying her immediate predecessor in the fleet, she is a catamaran and is, in effect, very similar to Wightline's *Wight Scene*. The *Ocean Scene's* arrival at Ocean Village followed financial problems both with her builders at Borth and with her future owners. However, she survived these difficult times and was completed at Ocean Village by the new owner of Blue Funnel, and subsequently slipped at Husband's Yard, Marchwood, prior to entering service.

Since 1992, the *Island Scene* has been on a long-term charter in the north-east, on the Tyne. During 1994, the Leisure Scene left Solent waters to start a new area of service for Blue Funnel, operating out of Poole. Thus, the new *Ocean Scene* was the only "Blue-Funneller" serving Southampton and it became necessary to charter the *Hythe Hotspur* which donned appropriate funnel colours for the summer duration.

An interesting husband-wife partnership, Mark and Jenny Rayment, has increasingly figured in Solent ferry and excursion work since 1968. Over the initial period of eight years, until 1976, three twelve-seater vessels were built, all three with the name of *Jenny Lee*. However, only one was in service at any time, each vessel being sold out of service on completion of her successor. The length of the craft was thirty-three feet.

So, at this early stage, the brand name of "Jenny" began, and it is common to hear the term "Jenny-boats" in conversation on both sides of the Solent, so familiar a part of the scene have their present day successors become.

In 1976, the Rayments broke their tradition and purchased a second-hand craft called the *Sparkle* (dating from 1946). This craft was somewhat larger at forty-six feet and had come from service in the West Country. She was subsequently renamed *Jenny Lee*.

The *Jenny Lee*, ex *Sparkle*, was destined to spend only one season on the Solent, that of the Jubilee year of 1977. She was sold for further service in Orkney, Scotland.

Her replacement was a forty feet fibreglass vessel, of about five years old, from South Wales. The Rayments completed much improvement work on her, including the fitting of a wheelhouse. She also took the name of *Jenny Lee* for the 1978 season. During the following year, this vessel was chartered for twenty-one days by the Department of Trade to act as stand-by vessel to the salvaging of the West German tanker *Tarpenbeck* (999 grt, dating from 1972) which had collided with the logistic landing ship *Sir Geraint* in fog off Selsey on 21st June. The *Tarpenbeck* capsized three days later and was towed into Sandown Bay, where she was righted on 15th July. Throughout this period, the *Jenny Lee* had to circle, the crippled tanker almost perpetually in order to keep away foolhardy sightseers and souvenir hunters. This charter was helpful in establishing the Jenny-boat business.

The year 1979 also marked the purchase of a former harbour launch from Plymouth; this was renamed the *Girl Alison* and used only for the following season. Like other vessels of the fleet, she was sold for further service elsewhere.

It was in 1980 that the current launches began to emerge, for an Aquastar hull was purchased and fitted out locally at St. Helens. She entered service in 1981 as the *Jenny Ann*. Two years later saw the sale of the *Jenny Lee* and a Cheverton 45 North

Kyle hull was acquired and then completed as the *Jenny R*.

Within a year, an identical hull was bought from Fairey Marine; this was completed as the (fourth) *Jenny Lee*, entering service in 1984. It is interesting to note that the *Jenny R* and the *Jenny Lee* remain to this day the smallest Class IV vessels on the DTI register. These two "Jennies" usually operate the Cowes - Calshot-Hamble-Warsash commuter run, early morning and late afternoon/early evening.

Dating from the early 1960s, the *Buccaneer* was purchased in 1986. She had previously been operating on the Sandbanks ferry, but had become surplus to requirements when that route changed hands. Licensed for seventy passengers, she was primarily involved on River Medina excursions. Her time in the fleet was short lived.

The *Buccaneer's* replacement came in the form of the *Jenny M*, based on a Cheverton seventeen metre hull, thus being the biggest "Jenny" built to date. She was completed during 1988, and entered service the following April. She regularly cruises in Solent waters.

Two larger vessels now grace the Wightline Cruises, the name under which the Rayments market their operations. In 1986, the *Solent Scene* was acquired from the Southampton-based Blue Funnel fleet, complete with their Isle of Wight operations. A partnership was drawn up between the two companies, easily recognisable by the identical and attractive blue, white and black funnel colours. This no longer exists as each company now has its own clearly defined area of operation.

The second large craft is the *Wight Scene*. Mark Rayment decided , in 1990, that the time was now appropriate to purchase a catamaran, this design having the advantage of large passenger accommodation both inside and outside. In conjunction with Blue Funnel, two vessels were ordered, one for each company. They were to be similar but far from identical and catering for a different market from each other.

Financial troubles plagued the builders, FL Steelcraft (near Borth on the Welsh coast). Eventually, in December 1991, administrative receivers were called in and, from February to June 1992, Mark Rayment and some of his employees had no option but to commute to the Welsh coast and finish the ship themselves!

Six further weeks of fitting out took place on the River Medina. Hard work has been rewarded and the ship has given excellent service, although her propellers have had to be changed twice in order to improve performance.

The *Wight Scene* is now the largest Island-based pleasure cruiser and is regularly to be seen at either of her principal moorings, at Ryde Pier or in the River Medina, ready to sail on excursions, charters and occasionally ferrying work. It is significant that she has been deemed worthy to deputise on Wightlink's catamaran route from Ryde to Portsmouth in the past. On this service, she has offered a more comfortable, leisurely crossing, more in the style of the *Brading* and her sisters when refreshments could be purchased and strolls around the decks were possible.

The arrival of the *Wight Scene* meant that the *Solent Scene* had to be put on the sales list. Perhaps fortunately, no buyer has emerged - fortunate, because there seems to be adequate employment for the two

Wight Line cruises ***Wight Scene*** pictured on a cruise of Portsmouth Harbour in May 1994. *(Eric Brett)*

larger craft. The *Solent Scene* emerged for the 1994 season minus her central funnel, an obvious dummy, and now simply sports two thin appropriately coloured exhaust stacks on either side.

All the six vessels are actively involved in Solent area business, from mundane employment acting as a replacement for the Cowes - East Cowes chain ferry (the current one being "Number 5") during its overhaul, when road traffic has to divert several miles inland via Newport, to late night crossings for special theatre trips. Portsmouth and Southampton are regular ports of call, the former now offering a special berth for the Wightline pleasure craft adjacent to the beautifully restored HMS *Warrior* and the main entrance to Portsmouth dockyard. Flexibility is very much the keynote of operations and this, coupled with the high rate of stability of the skippers and crews, has made this company one of the success stories of the Solent.

Although not based in the Solent, the Poole concern of Croson merits inclusion in this chapter on account of its operation to Yarmouth. Plugging the gap, left by the demise of Cosen's paddle steamer *Embassy* (formerly Southern Railways' *Duchess of Norfolk*, dating from 1911), at the end of the 1966 season, Croson acquired the *Coronia* from the Johnson family of Scarborough, Yorkshire. She had been built to the order of a Mr. Jack Ellis, first entering commercial service in 1935.

This ship began life with a striking profile of one flat-topped funnel (not unlike that of the pleasure cruiser, *Balmoral*), positioned rather more closely to the stern than was customary. During 1937, a forward, dummy funnel was added; this was, thankfully, removed during her was service.

The *Coronia* arrived at the Solent with a history more impressive than most of her Solent consorts, having operated cruises along the coast between Robin Hood's Bay (to the north) and Filey Bay (to the south). She could carry 472 passengers on her Class III certificate; they were frequently treated to the musical strains of a small band.

During the war years, the *Coronia* served on the Humber and in the Scottish Lochs. She saw service as a naval detention ship on the Tyne. Eventually, she was to serve in the Mediterranean, but the culmination of her achievements was, perhaps, her involvement as a tender in the Normandy Landings in 1944. The *Coronia* was part of the "Pluto" operation.

After the war, she was refitted and acquired a wheelhouse, replacing the open bridge. She resumed her pre-war sailings. In 1951, the Johnsons acquired her, on the death of Mr. Ellis. She not only continued her regular cruising pattern but added to her repertoire excursions to oil rigs, nearly twenty miles offshore.

The *Coronia* made her final cruise (to Robin Hood's Bay) in late September, 1967 and was sold to Croson Ltd. in May, 1968. On her arrival at Poole, she was renamed the *Bournemouth Queen* (a name recalling the much loved Red Funnel paddler of 1908 - 1957) and immediately became involved in the Poole, Bournemouth and Isle of Wight trade.

She remained with the company until October, 1974. During this time, she was a frequent voyager in the western reaches of the Solent, though occasional trips brought her further east, even into Portsmouth dockyard. Bringing day-trippers to the island, she was, effectively, a pleasure ferry, operating defined routes on a schedule. Although small by comparison to the last "big" cruise ferry in the area (the *Balmoral*, whose period of service overlapped that of the *Bournemouth Queen* by only a few months), she was sufficiently long, at nearly 130 feet, to look a substantial ship.

On the *Bournemouth Queen's* demise, she was sold to McAlpine and Sons, who renamed her the Queen of Scots. She was used for service on the Clyde, between Rothesay and Ardyne Point, and was largely involved in ferrying oil rig personnel. She operated occasional cruises and was chartered as a replacement for the paddle steamer Waverley during August, 1977, when the latter grounded on the Gantocks.

In 1978, she was sold again and continued to operate cruises in that area. Eventually, the former *Bournemouth Queen* was to sail south on retirement and she is now moored at Rochester where her former profile has been considerably changed in her new role as a restaurant.

This ship was very much a bridge between the old paddle steamers and the launches which are commonplace today. The firm of Croson is connected with Bolsons, the small ship builders and repairers, and it was to them that Croson turned to replace their ageing fleet with purpose-built craft.

The *Bournemouth Queen* was, effectively, replaced by the *Dorset Belle*, constructed in 1974. She has passenger accommodation for 196 and, at 46 grt, is considerably smaller than her successor (227 grt). A new age had begun. This vessel was a "mark I" version of the present two boats, the *Bournemouth Belle* (1975) and the *Poole Belle* (1977).

Eventually, the *Dorset Belle* was sold to Mursel and Kemp of Sandown (I.W.) who renamed her the *Island Enterprise*; she continues to give yeoman service in the Solent and round to Sandown Bay, ferrying trippers, football supporters and the like to and from the mainland, and to various Island destinations. She sports a very dark blue hull, which makes her easily distinguishable from her two near-sisters, whose current Croson livery is a very bright blue hull with cream upperworks.

The *Poole Belle* has more covered accommodation than her consort and so she is usually the vessel that ventures into Solent waters. Operating between May and October, Croson operates a day-ferry, giving half a day ashore.

Like her fleetmate, the *Poole Belle* was constructed to meet the demands of the prevailing economic climate. Her seating, arranged in bus-like fashion certainly smacks of a functional, yet reasonably comfortable, craft.

Croson has a working relationship with the Waverley Steam Navigation Company. When the latter's preserved vessels operate on the South Coast, Croson will sell tickets on their behalf.

By far the most spectacular and interesting coastal passenger cruise vessels visiting the Solent are the former LNER/Caledonian Macbrayne paddle steamer *Waverley* (dating from 1947) and the motor "yacht" *Balmoral*, built locally at Thornycroft's, Southampton, for Red Funnel in 1949. Operated by the Waverley Steam Navigation Company, which grew out of the Paddle Steamer Preservation Society, the paddler is constantly being restored and even upgraded to meet increasingly stringent DTI safety requirements. Furthermore, her operating schedules become more and more

A fine view of the preserved paddle steamer ***Waverley*** at Yarmouth in September 1989. *(R Sprake Collection)*

The faithful **Southsea** pictured arriving at Portsmouth in her last season on the Solent in 1988. *(Maritime Photographic)*

adventurous, bringing the pleasures of a sadly bygone age to people throughout the length and breadth of Britain, not to mention trips to Ireland and to within sight of the French coast.

The *Waverley* made her first visit to the Solent in April and May, 1978. In most years subsequently, she has circumnavigated the Isle of Wight (in both directions), operated from Portsmouth, Southsea, Ryde, Sandown, Yarmouth and Southampton en route to such places as Bournemouth, Poole, Swanage, and Weymouth to the west, and Littlehampton, Worthing, Brighton, Eastbourne and Folkestone to the east.

The paddle steamer is a large ship by Solent standards, almost matching the largest cross-Solent ferries, the paddle steamers *Southsea* and *Whippingham* (of 1930). The *Southsea* was a war loss, but the *Whippingham* lasted until 1962. With the charm and excitement of steam-driven, oil-fired engines driving the mighty paddle wheels, the *Waverley* has been a particularly welcome vessel on such occasions as the start of the Round-the-World Yacht Race in 1993 and the fiftieth anniversary of the Normandy D-Day Landings in June, 1994, when she joined, as did the *Balmoral*, the Fleet Review in the Solent.

Her varnished bridge frontal, her two tall funnels faithfully restored to her original LNER red, white and black give a taste of the delights below where the excursionist can witness the triple expansion engine in all its glory. The *Waverley* is considerably faster than most passenger vessels on the Solent. Her forward lounge, redesigned and considerably improved during the 1993/94 refit, is named after her elder half-sister, the *Jeanie Deans*.

The *Balmoral* was no stranger when she returned to the Solent as the *Waverley's* consort. Her survival, no doubt, is, in part at least, the result of the sad loss of the former Solent ferry and excursion vessel, *Shanklin*, which ended her days off the Gower peninsula in August, 1981.

The *Balmoral* operated for the first nineteen years of her life on the Red Funnel Southampton - West Cowes route, and on that company's cruising rosters, making her way round the Isle of Wight on hundreds of occasions. When she was replaced, in 1968, by the *Norris Castle* (which, incidentally, has now herself just been replaced by the *Red Osprey*), she served for many years on the Bristol Channel, operating throughout its length and breadth. Some occasional trips to the Scillies were also made. Her days based at Bristol came to an end in October, 1980. The *Balmoral* languished at Dundee as a far-from-successful floating restaurant until 1985.

Her purchase by a group of enthusiasts connected with the PSPS, followed by a complete refit during which the aft car deck was plated-in, so providing a very adequate dining saloon, brought a fast, versatile cruise ship of classic design to the coasts of Britain. Although based in Bristol, the *Balmoral* usually visits the Solent, her old stomping ground, each year. She provides similar cruises to those of the *Waverley* though her manoeuvrability and slightly shorter length has enabled her to undertake most unusual visits that her fleet companion cannot do. For example, she has sailed up the River Medina into the heart of Newport and she has tied up alongside the fragile Totland Pier which had not played host to a call by a pleasure steamer since 1966.

Unlike that of the *Waverley*, the *Balmoral's* livery has varied considerably over her years with the Waverley Steam Navigation Company. From 1986 until 1991, she sported a white profile, with green lining and a pale yellow funnel. Since then, her lower hull has been painted British Racing Green, with ivory above. The funnel seems regularly to change its colours, though the *Balmoral's* Solent admirers have strong preferences for either those of the *Waverley* or the original red and black with which she began life.

To the extreme west of the Solent, there is a small ferry route which operates from Keyhaven to Hurst Castle, though this is very much a seasonal service. The vessels are launches of approximately forty feet in length. They have limited covered accommodation, being primarily fair weather craft. They sport the names of *Wight Rose*, *Solent Rose*, *Island Rose* and *Haven Rose* and are operated, by the Hurst Castle Ferry Company.

Andrew Munn

This article has had to rely on information which is not always readily available. Small ferries and cruise ships have a habit of disappearing and then re-appearing where and when least expected. Even vessels the size of the Gosport ferries have "vanished".

FLEET INFORMATION

Above: Brittany Ferries ***Duchesse Anne*** captured in the evening sun arriving at Portsmouth from St. Malo. *(Maritime Photographic)*
Below: Hovertravel's ***Freedom 90*** sets off for the Isle of Wight on a busy summer's afternoon. *(Maritime Photographic)*

BRITTANY FERRIES

THE COMPANY *Brittany Ferries* is the trading name of BAI SA, a French private sector company and the operating arm of the *Brittany Ferries* group. The UK operations are run by *BAI (UK) Ltd*, a UK private sector company, wholly owned by the *Brittany Ferries Group*.

MANAGEMENT Group Managing Director: Christian Michielini, **Managing Director UK & Ireland:** Ian Carruthers, **Marketing Director:** David Longden.

ADDRESS The Brittany Centre, Wharf Road, PORTSMOUTH.

TELEPHONE Administration: 01705 827701, **Reservations:** 01705 827701.

ROUTES OPERATED Portsmouth – Santander (Spain) (winter only) (29 hrs – 33 hrs - 1 per week), St Malo – Portsmouth (8 hrs 45 mins (day), 9 hrs 30 mins – 10 hrs (night) - 1 per day), Caen (Ouistreham) – Portsmouth (6 hrs (day), 6 hrs – 7 hrs (night) - 3 per day).

VESSELS

BARFLEUR	*20500t	92	19k	1173P	550C	125T	BA	Helsinki, FI	FR
BRETAGNE*	23000t	89	21k	2030P	580C	40L	BA	St Nazaire, FR	FR
DUC DE NORMANDIE*	9355t	78	21k	1500P	350C	44T	BA	Heusden, NL	FR
DUCHESSE ANNE	6812t	79	20k	1300P	290C	39T	BA	Cork, IR	FR
NORMANDIE*	27000t	92	20k	2263P	630C	66T	BA	Turku, FI	FR
QUIBERON	8441t	75	20k	1302P	300C	35L	BA2	Rendsburg, GE	FR
VAL DE LOIRE*	31395t	87	21k	1800P	550C	114T	BA	Bremerhaven, GE	SW

*** Operates from Portsmouth**

COMMODORE FERRIES

THE COMPANY *Commodore Ferries Ltd* is a Guernsey private sector company.

MANAGEMENT Managing Director: Jeff Vidamour.

ADDRESS Commodore House, Bulwer Avenue, St Sampson's, GUERNSEY, Channel Islands GY2 4JN.

TELEPHONE Administration: 01481 46841 **Reservations:** 01481 46841. **Fax:** 01481 49543.

ROUTE OPERATED Portsmouth – Channel Islands (9 hrs - 3 per day).

VESSELS

COMMODORE CLIPPER	2311t	71	17k	12P	–	50T	A	Kristiansand, NO	NO
NORMAN COMMODORE	1577t	72	17k	12P	–	45T	BA	Florø, NO	BA
PURBECK	*3046t	78	17.5k	58P	–	64T	BA	Le Havre, FR	FR
ISLAND COMMODORE		95	18.3k	12P	–	95T	A	Vlissingen,NL	BA
NEWBUILDING		96	18.3k	12P	–	95T	A	Vlissingen,NL	BA

P&O EUROPEAN FERRIES

P&O
European Ferries

THE COMPANY *P&O European Ferries Ltd* is the trading name of *P&O European Ferries (Dover), P&O European Ferries (Portsmouth)* and *P&O European Ferries (Felixstowe)*, British private sector companies, part of the *P&O Group*. These companies were, until 1987, respectively: *Townsend Car Ferries, Thoresen Car Ferries* and *Atlantic Steam Navigation*, all part of *European Ferries* and trading as *Townsend Thoresen*. *European Ferries* was taken over by the *P&O Group* in January 1987 and the trading name was changed in October 1987.

MANAGEMENT (Portsmouth) Managing Director: Richard Martin, **Head Passenger Marketing & Sales :** Richard Kirkman.

ADDRESS Peninsular House, Wharf Road, PORTSMOUTH PO2 8TA

TELEPHONE Administration: 01705 772000 **Reservations:** 01705 827677

ROUTES OPERATED Portsmouth – Cherbourg 5 hours (day), 7 hours (night); - Up to 4 per day, Portsmouth – Le Havre 5hrs 30 mins (day), 7 hrs 30 mins (night) - 3 per day, Portsmouth – Bilbao (Spain) (35 hrs (UK-Spain), 30 hrs (Spain-UK) - 2 per week,

VESSELS

PRIDE OF BILBAO	37583t	86	22k	2500P	600C	90T	BA	Turku, FI	BA
PRIDE OF HAMPSHIRE	*14760t	75	18k	1200P	380C	50L	BA2	Ålborg, DK	GB
PRIDE OF LE HAVRE	*14760t	75	18k	1200P	380C	50L	BA2	Ålborg, DK	GB
PRIDE OF PORTSMOUTH	*33336t	90	21k	1600P	575C	118T	BA	Bremerhaven, GE	GE
PRIDE OF LE HAVRE	*33336t	89	21k	1600P	575C	118T	BA	Bremerhaven, GE	GE

RED FUNNEL

THE COMPANY *Red Funnel Ferries* is the trading name of the *Southampton Isle of Wight and South of England Royal Mail Steam Packet Public Limited Company*, a British private sector company. The company was acquired by *Associated British Ports* (owners of Southampton Docks) in 1989.

MANAGEMENT Managing Director: A M Whyte, **Marketing Director:** Ms O H Glass.

ADDRESS 12 Bugle Street, SOUTHAMPTON SO9 4LJ.

TELEPHONE Administration: 01703 333042, **Reservations:** 01703 330333, **Fax:** 01703 639438.

ROUTE OPERATED Southampton – East Cowes (55 mins; hourly).

1	RED FALCON	*3000t	94	13k	900P	140C	14L	BA	Port Glasgow, GB	GB
2	RED FALCON	*3000t	94	13k	900P	140C	14L	BA	Port Glasgow, GB	GB
3	NETLEY CASTLE	1184t	74	12k	786P	85C	16L	BA	Wallsend, GB	GB
4	NEWBUILDING	*3000t	94	13k	900P	140C	14L	BA	Port Glasgow, GB	GB

Red Funnel Ferries also operate two 67 passenger hydrofoils named the SHEARWATER 5 (62t, 1980) and the SHEARWATER 6 (62t, 1982) and two 130 passenger catamarans named the RED JET 1 (168t, 1991) and the RED JET 2 (168t, 1991). They operate between Southampton and West Cowes; journey time is 20 minutes.

STENA SEALINK LINE

THE COMPANY *Stena Sealink Line* is the trading name of *Stena Sealink Ltd*, a British private sector company. It was purchased (as *Sealink UK Ltd*) from the state owned *British Railways Board* in summer 1984 by *British Ferries Ltd*, a wholly owned subsidiary of *Sea Containers* of Bermuda. In 1990 most services and vessels were purchased from *Sea Containers* by *Stena Line AB* of Sweden – although the Isle of Wight vessels and services were excluded. In late 1990 the trading name was changed to *Sealink Stena Line* and in 1993 changed to *Stena Sealink Line*. *Stena Line* is named after its founder, Sten A Olsson.

MANAGEMENT Managing Director: W Gareth Cooper, **Marketing Director:** John Govett.

ADDRESS Charter House, Park Street, ASHFORD, Kent TN24 8EX.

TELEPHONE Administration: 01233 647022, **Reservations:** 01233 647047.

ROUTE OPERATED Southampton – Cherbourg (5 hrs (day), 8-9hrs (night) - 1 or 2 per day.

VESSEL

11	STENA NORMANDY	17043t	82	20.4k	2100P	480C	52L	BA2	Göteborg, SW	BA

WIGHTLINK

THE COMPANY *Wightlink* is a British private sector company, part of the *Sea Containers* group. The routes and vessels were previously part of *Sealink* but were excluded from the purchase of most of the *Sealink* operations by *Stena Line AB* in 1990.

MANAGEMENT Managing Director: Mel Williams, **Marketing Manager:** R I Stewart.

ADDRESS PO Box 59, PORTSMOUTH PO1 2XB.

TELEPHONE Administration: 01705 812011, **Reservations:** 01705 827744, **Fax:** 01705 855257, **Telex:** 86440 WIGHTLG.

ROUTES OPERATED Lymington – Yarmouth (Isle of Wight) (30 mins; half hourly), Portsmouth – Fishbourne (Isle of Wight) (35 mins; half hourly/hourly).

VESSELS

1	CAEDMON	761t	73	9.5k	756P	58C	6L	BA	Dundee, GB	GB
2	CENRED	761t	73	9.5k	756P	58C	6L	BA	Dundee, GB	GB
3	CENWULF	761t	73	9.5k	756P	58C	6L	BA	Dundee, GB	GB
4	ST CATHERINE	*2036t	83	12.5k	1000P	142C	12L	BA	Leith, GB	GB
5	ST CECILIA	*2968t	87	12.5k	1000P	142C	12L	BA	Selby, GB	GB
6	ST FAITH	*2968t	90	12.5k	1000P	142C	12L	BA	Selby, GB	GB
7	ST HELEN	*2983t	83	12.5k	1000P	142C	12L	BA	Leith, GB	GB

Wightlink also operate two passenger only high speed catamarans – the OUR LADY PATRICIA and the OUR LADY PAMELA – between Portsmouth and Ryde. They are of 312 tons, were built in 1986 in Tasmania, Australia, seat 406 passengers, cruise at 28.5k and are British registered.

OTHER SOLENT COMPANIES

Gosport Ferry GOSPORT QUEEN (159t, 1966, 550 passengers), PORTSMOUTH QUEEN (159t, 1966, 500 passengers), SOLENT ENTERPRISE (274t, 1971, 500 passengers (ex GAY ENTERPRISE)). **Route operated:** Gosport – Portsmouth.

Hovertravel DOUBLE-O-SEVEN (1989, 96 passengers), FREEDOM 90 (1990, 96 passengers) **Route operated:** Southsea-Ryde

KEY TO FLEET INFORMATION

List of vessels

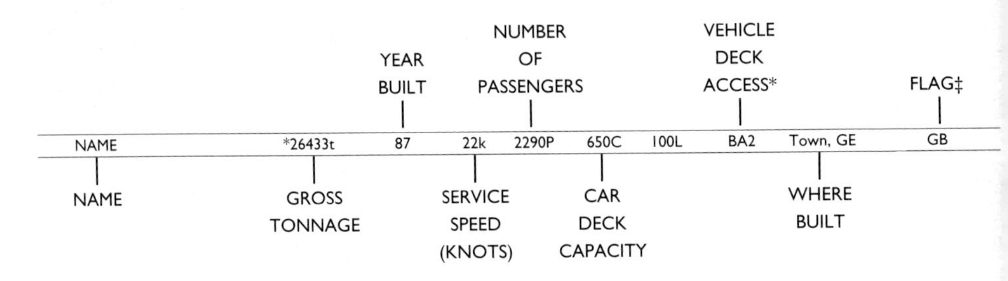

* B=Bow/A=Aft

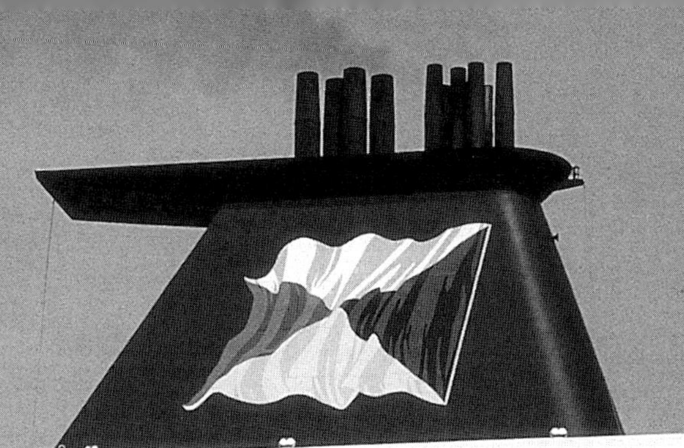

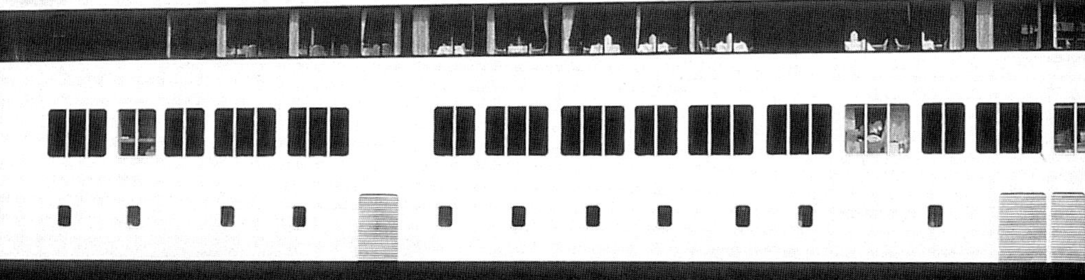

P&O

Pride of Portsmouth *(Miles Cowsill)*

FURTHER READING

Title	Author(s)	Date
British Channel Island Ferries	Miles Cowsill	1989
Brittany Ferries 1973-1993	Miles Cowsill	1994
Earl William (History of Thoresen & Sealink ferry)	Miles Cowsill	1990
Ferries of the English Channel	Miles Cowsill & John Hendy	1993
Hoverspeed Story, The (2nd edition)	Miles Cowsill & John Hendy	1993
Inside Olau	Alan Oligvie	1994
P&O European Ferries, The Fleet (3rd edition)	Miles Cowsill & John Hendy	1992
Sealink Stena Line, The Fleet	Miles Cowsill & John Hendy	1992
Townsend Thoresen Years,The (2nd edition)	Miles Cowsill & John Hendy	1987
Viking Saga, The (Cherbourg & Le Havre)	Miles Cowsill & John Hendy	1989
Wightlink (Isle of Wight Ferries)	John Hendy	1993

All published by Ferry Publications

TO KEEP IN TOUCH WITH THE FERRY WORLD YOU NEED

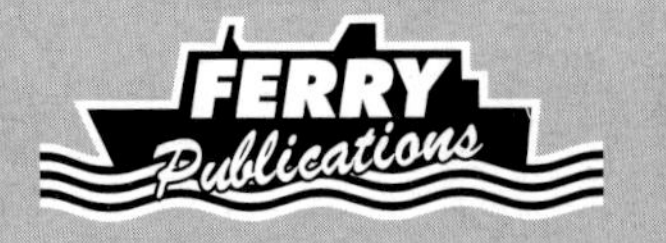

BRITISH FERRY SCENE

Our quarterly magazine is packed with facts, photographs and details of everything that's going on in the world of British ferries. The 56 pages are eagerly awaited by both enthusiasts and those who work in the industry. If you're interested in ferries then this magazine is a MUST!

Annual subscription £10.90 (UK), £12.50 (Europe & Eire), Overseas: £13.80 .

Available from:- Ferry Publications, 12 Millfields Close, Kilgetty, Pembrokeshire, SA68 0SA

Tel: (01834) 813991 Fax: (01834) 814484